A BRIEF INHALATION

I0564175

Daragh Fleming is a writer from Cork, Ireland. He has work published in many literary magazines, including *Stand, Southword,* and *Crannóg*. He was shortlisted for the Alpine Fellowship Poetry Prize in 2024, and highly commended for both the Patrick Kavanagh Award and the Fool For Poetry Prize in 2023. He won the Duncairn Flash Competition in 2024. This is his second collection of essays.

Also by Daragh Fleming

Lonely Boy   (Book Hub, 2022)

Notes for a Mid-youth Crisis   (Bottlecap Press, 2022)

If You Are Reading This Then Drink Water   (Riversong Books, 2020)

The Book of Revelations   (Riversong Books, 2019)

PRAISE for *A Brief Inhalation*

A Brief Inhalation is Cork-born poet, essayist and activist Daragh Fleming's warm, meditative and often laugh-out-loud funny treatise on grief, loss, discomfort and coming-of-age. Covering subjects as diverse as the strange and melancholy beauty of inherited clothing, inner city skateboarding, ADHD, childhood snake rearing, the world of social (and anti-social) media, and all too brief interludes with mysterious strangers who leave lasting impressions, Fleming, with trademark wit and honesty weaves his way from his home in Ireland on travels through Barcelona, Prague, London and Lyon observing new and unfamiliar locales through the eyes of an outsider searching for connection. Part creative manifesto, part travelogue, part personal memoir, there are shades of early Richard Linklater in these tales of missed romantic opportunity and youthful misadventure with a roll call of unforgettable characters who leap off the page.
— Lucy Holme

These diary-like episodes show Fleming's fearlessness, exposing his young heart's frailties and transgressions with the art and honesty of a poet.
— Paul McVeigh

A Brief Inhalation is a book that you will, as the title demands, inhale as Daragh fumbles his way, disarmingly, through Europe and his emotions. Reminding you with every carefully chosen word, every cautionary tale, that the only person who can save you is you.
— Kate Durrant

Throughout the impactful, soul-baring essays in *A Brief Inhalation*, Daragh Fleming shares with the reader personal experiences ranging from the sublime to the surreal. With a twist of deadpan humour and a poetic sensibility, he harnesses a tender honesty to write about navigating love and friendship in the digital age, the trials of burgeoning sexuality and finding connection among strangers abroad. This is a deeply human and intimate collection of memories, ruminations and revelations, penned by a writer whose greatest strength is his willingness to be vulnerable in a world that doesn't always reward vulnerability.
— Aoife Barry

For my mother, Catherine, who knew I'd be doing this long before I, or anyone else, had any notion.

ISBN: 978-1-916938-87-8

Cover designed by Aaron Kent

Cover image: © Olena / Adobe Stock

Edited and Typeset by Aaron Kent

Broken Sleep Books Ltd
PO BOX 102
Llandysul
SA44 9BG

CONTENTS

Now I am quietly waiting for
the catastrophe of my personality
to seem beautiful again,
and interesting, and modern.

— Frank O' Hara, *Mayakovsky*

A Brief Inhalation

Daragh Fleming

Broken Sleep Books

NOTE #1

Once upon a time I was born and then I was dying. Umbilical cord around my neck, it looked like an early exit from a brief life.

But then I wasn't. The doctor sorted me out. I was being dramatic. But I was a baby so that's to be expected. My tongue was tied, but otherwise I seemed grand. Just a very un-notable baby in quite an extraordinary world. Classic case of hurtling into existence.

I was a shy boy. I got embarrassed quite easily. I was afraid to talk to people I didn't know. And at the beginning you don't know almost everyone. But with people I knew and was comfortable with, I was very open. My brother was my best friend and my worst enemy all rolled into one tiny, blonde person. My mother and father were dead on. They gave me food and a bed and toys the entire way up.

As I got older, I got less shy but more fat. I ate a lot. I loved sweets, hated cheese, and enjoyed everything else in between. I was plump. It was described as puppy fat, being big boned. Something I'd grow out of. Which made sense as I'd grown into it. But that was my own doing, so I concluded that I'd have to be the one to instigate the growing-out-of too. I hated most sports. Didn't understand them. That was, until I found basketball and thought it was the most perfect sport anyone could ever play. Once that happened, I started the growing-out-of process. I got taller and less fat—although I'd forever consider myself to be fat afterwards because I had come to believe that I could never not be fat. I grew into my ears that were, up until then, bizarrely disproportionate to the rest of my head.

Girls didn't like me for a long time but then, at some stage, they did start liking me. I was out of the universal friendzone. This was knowledge that changed me. The shyness all but gone, at sixteen I was dating. And then I got my heartbroken. And then my best friend killed himself.

And then I was stuck for the first time really, bar a few micro-moments prior to that. I got stuck. Depressed and untrusting. I wouldn't open up to anyone in any real way for probably another ten years after that. I was seventeen. My route into stuckness was severe and traumatic.

I was emotionally numb for five years. Five years of emotionless, painless, lifeless fun. I tried lots of things to jump start my emotions.

I had a lot of sex. That never worked. I always thought the next time would be different but I always came away feeling nothing but tired, empty. And my partners couldn't understand it because I didn't understand it enough to communicate it effectively. So they left. And I knew I should have felt upset about that but I didn't feel anything. I wanted them to stay while also feeling no way different about their leaving.

I drank. I was in college for most of this stuck part so it didn't appear out of the ordinary. I got on the cans, the pints, the bottles, the whiskey, the vodka. When I was drunk I was able to feel things. It felt nice to feel things. So I got drunk when I could, when my schedule allowed it. Which brings me onto my next point—

I got busy. I played basketball on four different teams. I had two jobs. I was at college. I consumed information, played video games, went on nights out. I did everything I could not to spend time on my own because, if I did that, I'd have to acknowledge that something was off.

I didn't cause myself to become stuck. But I was stuck longer than I had to be because I didn't want to accept it. I dragged it out because I was scared. Scared of feeling broken. Scared of being seen as broken. I could have gotten myself loose long before I did.

But this is the thing about being stuck—when you're in it, you don't have any desire to pull yourself out of it.

A BRIEF INHALATION

Wind. Like the propellers of ancient aircraft. But not propelled. Wind in my ears. Suffocating volume. Noise-cancelling wind. Beautiful, full absorption. Dry nose like a tea towel. Dry eyes like dry ice. Screaming but not hearing it. Screaming silently but feeling it. Gorgeous wind.

Scent of water. Salting, fizzy ocean. Far below, but in the nostril still. Rocks jagged in isolation. Stay away from here. Warning sings. *Private property, trespassers well be persecuted.* You shouldn't be here. Seagulls floating, gliding, thriving. Held up by the enormous, invisible gush of the world. The instinctive trust. The genetic understanding.

The wind breaks. A brief inhalation.

White noise of the ocean waving crashes in. Briefly. Exhalation. Omnipresent wind. Never relenting, just changing position.

Here you go, it says, *hear me go.*

Hands and arms splayed out, stretched out, trying to catch either side of the sky and fold it in on itself. Keep it safe until tomorrow. Wind on bare skin. This is how you're meant to feel it. Shoulder-blades pulled apart like seams of grass. Chest like a cave opening up below. Let the water inside. Allow it make ancient sounds against the hollows of your cavern.

See the edge. Feel the edge. Fear the edge. Edge of the world.

Edge of someone else's horizon. Grass about the edge like someone tore up the carpet. Bad-haircut grass. Careless barber scissor-hands. Miles of hairy continent and then suddenly—none.

The wind now, like a friend, egging you on. Edging you to the edge. Gentle sway, firm push.

Here you go, it says, *here we go.*

Eyes closed. Ears covered. Nose masked. Skin, alive. Deep gulp of godly wind. Trust it like the seagull. Understand genetically.

Leave go, it says, *leave you go.*

TO OLOT WITH LOVE

In the northeast of Spain, about two hours by bus north of Barcelona, there is a small town called Olot. Nestled among dormant volcanoes and mountains and streams, it is a quiet town. There's not much going on here; it is a normal place filled with normal people living normal lives. Away from the buzz of city life in Barcelona, people lead slower lives here. Buses leave on the hour, retired men and women stroll around the town centre, dogs walk without their leashes. And yet it is also a town that draws people from every corner of the map, somehow. Hikers and writers and musicians and teachers and poets and actors and salesman and travellers. They come from all around the world to play and write and walk and live.

But more pertinent than that, people are drawn to Olot for love.

I can't quite articulate it, but I can feel it. There is a certain quality to the air. A stillness that whispers, encouraging connection. I am here as a writer, to work on a book that refuses to be finished. But as the days trickle past I can feel this town's presence causing the most unlikely of people to find one another. There's an unknowable force flowing through the streams and rustling in the trees. I can feel it, and I also meet other people who have felt it, who have settled in Olot for decades exactly for this reason. Called from faraway lands across nation's borders they came, all for something as unreliable as love.

Marina, for example, came from Russia. She works as a language teacher in the local language school teaching Russian and English. She's a quiet woman but her story stays with me because it feels unfathomable in our modern world. As we sit for dinner in the main town square she recalls what drew her to Olot to begin with.

"Back then the internet was this confusing thing. I considered signing up for email but didn't think I'd ever use it. I joined a chat room for learning languages. I wanted to learn Spanish, but they said to write the advertisements in either English or Russian. I ignored this and decided to write mine in what little Spanish I knew."

From there a man reached out and they became pen-pals, first with letters and then (reluctantly) through email.

"I remember some time later he told me he chose me because mine was the only ad written in Spanish."

From their intent to learn language blossomed an innocent love. Love that coiled through the abstract unknown internet between Russia and Spain. Back and forth messages went, the connection growing deeper with each one sent. Eventually Marina decided she'd go along to Spain to meet her boyfriend-to-be. But her parents had different ideas.

"Even though I was 19, my father wouldn't let me go. I craved independence, but he thought it too dangerous for a young woman.

They were different times. I was really disappointed."

When she told her pen-pal the news however, he said that he'd come to Russia instead to meet her, much to her delight. And to Russia he came. Despite Marina's father insisting on coming to the airport to collect him, again interrupting Marina's desire to be an independent woman, he came and stayed in a nearby hotel. And so it seemed that Marina's future was solidified.

Marina finished out her degree in Russia, and a few years later moved to Olot in Spain, eventually to marry her pen-pal, and to live there ever since.

This story is one of many, but it speaks to a sort of non-religious faith that no longer exists. A trust that is banished from today's world. An unshaking belief in a stranger is almost unthinkable now, but for Marina—for love back then—it was often entwined with finding it.

And now she's been in Olot for almost thirty years, married happily to a man who was once a stranger on the internet.

Marina was working in the same language school when another woman named Carol arrived from America. Carol, an archetype of the Hippy Movement of the sixties, also came to Olot for romantic love, but stayed because of her love of place.

When I meet Carol first she is direct, her accent a thick generic American. She is happy to meet me and is full of chat. She drinks bottled beer and smokes damp, hand-rolled cigarettes. She wears a thousand colours and is perpetually up for adventure. Her hair is long and grey, but her eyes are brimming with life. So it is unsurprising that, once Marina has told us her tale of love, Carol tells us hers, too.

Hers is a different story entirely. Coming to Olot thirty-three years previous, she wanted to introduce her son to her husband's family who lived nearby. Eventually her marriage broke down but Carol stayed having fallen for the lifestyle on offer in the quiet countryside of Catalunya. She lived, unemployed and free, in a variety of farmhouses throughout the region for years.

Carol lived what I'd describe as an adventurous life. Giving birth to four children from four different men, Carol was a liberated woman in an era where feminine liberation was looked down upon, and frankly, discouraged and forbidden. When we talk she mentions that at one point her daughter's classmates referred to Carol as a whore. When her daughter told her this she responded, "No I'm not. I didn't get paid for any of it." And that was the end of that.

I like Carol a lot.

As well as mothering four children, Carol spent fourteen years in a cult based vaguely around a Christian belief system. Two of her children were born during this time, adding to the total membership of one hundred within the cult. No children were ever birthed in a hospital, yet there were no mortalities within the fourteen years, which Carol referred to as a miracle in itself. However, when the cult eventually split up, many of the children struggled to assimilate back into mainstream society, which resulted in a string of tragic suicides.

The cult went global, travelling from The States, to Mexico, Spain, and eventually, Israel. Carol mentions a brief stay in prison whilst they were situated in Mexico but doesn't say much further than that.

The cult eventually disbanded in Israel in 1988. The cult leader was adamant that the world would end the same year which came to be untrue, as you know, and so the devoted followers decided it was time for a fresh start. But for Carol, "Our world as we knew it did come to an end," giving me the sense that her belief didn't die when the cult did.

After this Carol found her way to Olot where she's been ever since—serving as a language teacher, nude model, and purveyor of the arts in general. Although the love she followed here has long since disappeared, a love of place has taken over. The culture of small town Catalunya suits her, as she sits in the terrace alongside me sipping from a bottle of beer, trying to get her rolled cigarette to light.

Both Marina and Carol come from vastly different worlds. Marina, from the repressive suffocation of old Russia. Carol, from the liberated Hippy era that defined a generation. And yet, they find themselves here in Olot, two unlikely friends, inseparable. Although they came here for romantic love in the first instance, it's clear that the love which has endured most concretely for both of them is platonic love and friendship.

Two completely different worlds, intertwined and flourishing in the unsuspecting town of Olot.

THE ART OF FALLING

Just on the edge of the El Raval neighbourhood in Barcelona, not far from La Rambla, the Museum of Contemporary Art (MACBA) resides. It stands defiantly, a modern building in an ancient place. El Raval is an area of the city that tourists are warned against entering alone, for this is where the more dangerous and adventurous of the city are said to reside. Pickpockets lurk in shadows and gangs of faceless men patrol with tattooed arms and dangerous eyes. Laneways are narrow and cobbled, shop fronts are shaded from the bleating sun. Restaurant owners encourage potential customers inside with pictures of patatas bravas and paella. This part of the city is as alive as all the other neighbourhoods, but it has an edgier quality to it. There is a sense of realness here, but also a sense of danger. Warnings from locals are persistent: "do not go there alone," they say. A caution for certain, but perhaps also a gauntlet laid down.

It might strike you as a strange setting for a contemporary art museum. There are far more touristic parts of the city after all. Places that feel more safe. Places that are less daunting to wander in to. There are more appropriate settings for sure. But to me it is the perfect location. Situated here in the volatile heart of the city stands a temple of modern creation. For it is from the real, gritty parts of life that art inevitably emerges.

So, if you wish to take in some of this art you must brave El Raval, navigating narrow alleyways that criss-cross like spiders webs. Patting pockets regularly to ensure the safety of belongings. And then it emerges, a colossal, modern building in the centre of one of Barcelona's oldest neighbourhoods. White in colour and reminiscent of a spaceship, the MACBA houses some of the modern era's most extraordinary art; tapestries of varying colour, geometrical paintings that send you on natural psychedelic trips, bizarre videos that leave the mind confused, strange rooms filled with gigantic sculptures with distorted versions of acid rock music videos projected silently on the walls. MACBA is a worthy expedition for anyone finding themselves in the core of Catalunya, leaving you wondering what exactly that was all about, and often provoking a craving for an extended trip into psychedelia. Even uttering the abbreviation 'MACBA' leaves one with a certain mystic aftertaste. It feels like a mantra. The building itself vibrates with the same sort of energy.

However, it is not the contemporary art on offer that has me captivated as I wait for my friend to arrive. There is another form of art linked to this museum, but it has nothing to do with what's inside. Outside MACBA there is a vast courtyard renowned for another contemporary endeavour—skateboarding. First discovered in California in the 1950s, skateboarding today is synonymous with alternative living. Much like the Hippy Movement of the 1960s, skateboarding points to a subsection of a generation trying to find a new path in a world that doesn't feel like home. And this movement is as prevalent in the capital city of Catalunya as anywhere.

Here, young skaters gather in throngs to test out their latest moves, video record perfected ones, and generally practice their craft in a place that has become synonymous with the contemporary culture of skateboarding in Barcelona. They endure grazed knees, shredded palms, fails, falls, trips and exhaustion in the pursuit of singular perfect moments. I am transported back to childhood summers spent along the coastline of Waterford where raw skin scabbed to the rhythm of this same desire for satisfaction. There is something deeply human about failing over and over with the hope of success on the ever-moving horizon.

As I stand on the opposite side of the courtyard from the main entrance to MACBA, the evening's sun still hot as hell, with sweat pooling in the small of my back, I try to plan a route through the hundreds of skaters buzzing around the courtyard like frantic bees. In front of me, a young man stands in the road to stop traffic, as several of the more experienced skaters in the community attempt high-flying acrobatic tricks by jumping from the top of the steps that lead to the museum. Despite their obvious expertise, almost none of these more brave skaters land these difficult manoeuvres successfully, and so they come crashing to the floor, after descending what has to be at least a 15 foot drop, landing then in the middle of a pedestrian crossing where cars should be zooming up and down. This, I am explicitly aware of, is not for the faint of heart.

They pick themselves up only to attempt the same tricks again, only to fall again. It is an exhibition of pure persistence, and it has me—one of its only audience members—absolutely absorbed.

It strikes me that these people are not only expert skaters; they are also professional fallers. Meaning they know how to fall from gut-wrenching heights without getting hurt. Men and woman skate and leap and fall perfectly. Their bodies automatically going limp, tumbling onto the ground like bananas, their spines adjusting to the contour of the ground, allowing them to go from free fall to back roll to standing position. They remain fluid rather than rigid, allowing them to fall repeatedly while taking on minimal damage. I think about how I would fall from these attempts—palms outstretched, knees clunky and forcefully hitting the concrete. Blood would stain my t-shirt and sweat would sting in open grazes. These skaters don't draw any blood when they crash. I know for certain that my knees and palms would resemble the frontline of an unnecessary war. My elbows would cut and bulge with bruises undoubtedly. There is a skill to falling well, and the skaters of Barcelona are masters of this craft.

As I stand and watch, waiting for my friend to arrive from her shift at the hospital, I realize that twenty minutes have passed in seconds. I am enthralled, hypnotised by the courageous attempts of these skaters as they leap again and again to complete a manoeuvre that is seemingly undoable. I know that even if I jumped from the top of those steps without a skateboard I would likely injure myself. But they don't. They soar and crash and brush themselves off and try again. Determination is key here. It is respected above all else. The best among them are simply those who keep showing up, who refuse to take failure as final.

The city evidently doesn't share my adoration for these artists. Each evening around 6:30PM several squad cars come blazing into the courtyard all blue and red, on a mission to intimidate and disperse. Sirens blare and skaters scatter. Although it is unlikely that arrests will be made, it is not worth tempting fate. Police officers approach and berate anyone who dares to linger after their arrival. There is an unspoken understanding. The city sees this unofficial skate park as heresy. It is a sore in the heart of the city. This place is reserved for modern art. Yet they do not understand that what these skaters are doing is an artform in itself.

My friend eventually arrives. She is just finished a shift from the hospital but insists on seeing the museum. Her eyes don't light up for the skaters like mine do. She is more concerned with the society-approved art. As we enter MACBA to take in the art I find it difficult to pull my mind away from what's going on outside. Inside we can still hear the slaps of wooden boards hitting concrete, of rubber wheels rolling upon the rough terrain, and the constant shouts of encouragement and laughter. I find myself in a museum with some of the most sought after art in the world but all I can focus on is the unvalidated artform taking place in real time just metres away.

Tapestries and paintings are beautiful, but they pale in comparison to the resilience of the human spirit, of the ability to keep getting up after we have fallen. I think this is what is so captivating about what happens just outside the MACBA. Talented as they are, what draws me to the skaters of Barcelona is their endurance, they reluctance to give up. Out there on the barren courtyard from dawn until dusk they hone their skills and attempt tricks that most of the world will never truly care for.

But this hardly matters. It is something they care about. They, like all other artists, are creating for the sake of creating. They are drawn to it the way we are drawn to words, the way painters are drawn to canvas. It is not for recognition nor validation that they swarm here. I imagine they would care less about it if the city approved. This is their art in the truest sense of the word. It is their revolt, their way of saying that they do not fit in and they do not wish to. For art that has conformed is no longer art. It is something else, something commercial. So they refuse to conform, and they accept that the police will come and arrest them and degrade them. But this makes the art more sweet, more pure, more meaningful.

And so if you go to Barcelona on any given day you'll find them there. Toiling away with cramped calves and tired thighs, creating art in motion, falling down and getting back up until the cops arrive.

When we finish up in MACBA the sun is already setting. The

skaters have already been dispersed, and now restaurant owners are setting up outdoor seating for the night ahead. I'd hoped to catch more of their acrobatic attempts, but their time is up. At least now I know where to find them—beneath this house of art, perfecting the art of falling.

A SNAKE NAMED SNAKE

My dad bought me a snake when I was eleven. He came into the mobile home, it shook as his weight was acknowledged. I was eating cereal near the front of the cab, sunlight streaming through the lace curtains. Every caravan seemed to have these lace curtains, covering the windows, an attempt at seeming posh and private, like we were all in denial over living in mobile homes.

My dad came in, I hadn't seen him all week because he'd been back in the city working. He came in with purpose, a smile on his face, knowledge behind the smile.

'I got you a surprise,' he said, waiting for me to look up. Every child lives for a good surprise and I was no different. I was lit up, already on my feet, clawing at his jumper for him to tell me what it was. I had no idea. It was nowhere near my birthday, nowhere near Christmas. I hadn't done anything, that I could remember, which deserved a surprise. A surprise was rare, not something that just landed at your feet every other day.

Eventually he revealed it to me.

'I got you a snake.'

'A snake?' I didn't know what to do with this information. We already had a dog. My hamster had died a few years before. Our dog was named Holly, she was a lovely terrier looking thing. We used to have a bird and a few fish, but they all died. And I wasn't really in the market for a new pet. But I was getting one, regardless.

'Yeah, just like your cousin, remember?'

I did remember. He wasn't really my cousin though, but rather my father's cousin. So although he was technically my cousin, he didn't feel like one. My cousins were other children I could play with, who lived in other caravans not far up the park. This cousin he was referring to was a full grown adult, with tattoos all over, no hair, and an accent you can only get if you live in England. He didn't feel like my cousin.

'Oh yeah... okay... is it here?' I was suddenly nervous as the reality of it set in.

The cousin in question had visited before the summer, to see my nana and grandad. He'd been intimidating, this colossal man with all the tattoos and the strange sounding voice. But I was curious, he was so different to any other adult in my life, that I'd been mesmerised. He started telling me about these giant snakes he owned, big slimy anacondas that were bigger than I was. I couldn't believe it, that someone—anyone—could have a snake as a pet. My parents, grandparents, all laughed at my disbelief, my fascination. And then my cousin went home and I forgot all about him and the snakes. But my father hadn't.

'Yes, he's out in the van. Come on, we'll take a look.'

I suppose, looking back, I can understand my father's confusion. Why he thought I'd like to have a snake of my own is reasonable.

A few years before, we went on a family trip to Dublin Zoo. It was my first time staying in a hotel. I remember that it felt like a fairy-tale, the way the beds were made so perfectly, and how you had a special card to get into the room, and the way the room smelt like nothing. All four of us shared the same room, me and my brother reluctantly sharing a double bed. At the zoo, I had begged to go to the reptile house to see the snakes and lizards, and when we were leaving I was allowed to buy something, so I chose a stuffed black and yellow snake, which I brought to bed with me every night, and which I eventually donated to one of the dogs when I get older.

And then of course, there was my childhood-obsession with the movie Godzilla, which wasn't about a snake, but rather a giant lizard, and my ongoing boyhood fascination with dinosaurs and anything to do with them. Putting the pieces together, it makes total sense that my dad would think that I'd love to own my very own, very real, snake.

But the truth is, I liked these things from afar. And the fascination was most likely rooted in a healthy fear. I found them interesting because a lot of them were poisonous, most of them would kill me given the opportunity. I didn't want to be near them, or have one to look after. I essentially thought they were cool for the same reason every boy thinks things are cool—because they were dangerous, and not a part of the world I existed in. There were no snakes native to Ireland, and dinosaurs were no longer real things, so I could have a blossoming obsession without ever having to cross paths with one, without ever having to prove I was brave enough to harbour such a curiosity. Until the day my father gifted me a corn-snake.

It was a gesture of good-will. I know this. An attempt to bond us, bring us closer together. My father found it much easier to connect with my older brother. Cillian was, is, more hands-on. Likes getting stuck in, helping with DIY projects, manual labour efforts, like cutting trees and painting fences. I was always far more reluctant, did these things out a sense of masculine obligation rather than an actual interest. Cillian was more typically a boy, a conceptual symbol my father could wrap his head around easier. I was probably always a little harder to decipher, more vague. Sensitive, uninterested in things like football and loud machines in the garden. The snake therefore, was some mad experience for us to share. Here's a monster that we have to look after together, my son. Because my mother was having none of it, and I made sure my brother knew the snake was my possession, even though I didn't really want it myself. Later, when I started playing basketball, this tied us together. We finally found something boyish and normal to connect us. But before that, there was the snake.

My dad produced a small glass box from the back of his van. Inside it was a chunk of tree, placed upon a bed of small stones. I couldn't see anything else initially, until I squinted and saw it -its skin blending in with the stones, about six inches in length, a pattern of browns and dark oranges, lying so still that I wasn't sure it was alive. A snake—my snake—existing in a small box, unaware that I existed.

There were many instructions to remember. He wasn't poisonous, so bites would hurt but would not be fatal. He would get bigger (I wasn't sure if it was a male or female snake but in my mind he was a boy because I was a boy) and we would need to get a bigger container from the pet shop to house him. We'd need heat lamps and heat mats because the snake would die if he got too cold. We had to buy bags of frozen mice, store them in our freezer, and feed him once a week. He'd shed his skin and we'd have to remove it. I remember the first time we took the skin out, being careful and quick so that the snake wouldn't bite my hand. I held the scroll of scaly skin, a tube of the snake's past in my hands, and wondered what to do with it (Eventually this became a normal occurrence and I simply threw them in the bin). I had to name him, but I settled on calling him 'Snake' as he didn't appear to respond to a name, and I didn't feel any strong emotional connection to him—I was fascinated, but there was no real love for this animal.

We fed him almost immediately—my father had stocked up on frozen mice to get us through the first month. The dead mouse felt bony in my hand, its pink face asleep, and I felt sad for needing to kill mice in order to sustain my new pet. I placed the mouse away from the snake's head, not wanting his attention, and waited. It took him almost an hour before he trained his attention on the dead mammal, and I watched in horror, in hypnosis, as Snake began the slow process of dislocating his own jaw in order to swallow his dinner whole. In this early stage, the mouse was far bigger than he was, and I couldn't understand how he was able to slowly absorb the mouse. When he was finished, he moved much slower, the mouse a very evident lump in his narrow body, which now resembled a blocked cartoon pipe, ready to erupt at a moment's notice.

It didn't take long for me to realise I would never pick this animal up. I was too afraid of its cold, reptilian movements, the way it couldn't show affection. I'd picked up dogs and cats and hamsters, all three of which acknowledged your existence either by cuddling closer to, or struggling to get away from, you. My dad had dried in blood and two parallel pinpricks on his left hand when he brought the snake inside, evidence that the snake had bitten him when he picked it up in the shop. So I knew that Snake already had a taste for our family's blood, and whether that made sense or not was irrelevant—I wasn't going to pick him up.

Snake grew quickly, lengthening and thickening. Although it wasn't always easy to gauge how big or small he was. He could contort, contract, expand, elongate, not dissimilar to the way an octopus moves. So, despite a general knowledge that I knew he was growing, I was never too certain how big he was.

We left our summer mobile home in August, travelling back to Cork from Waterford, snake-in-box tucked somewhere where it wouldn't topple over in the car. My mother hated having the thing, terrified I might, accidentally or otherwise, release the snake into our house to slither and slip between the furniture, appearing deadly in warm cupboards, foraging for food. But I never did accidentally leave him out, because I only opened his container when absolutely necessary.

Not long after we settled back into Cork, the new school year upon us, it became clear that Snake needed a new container to inhabit. He was getting too big, now resembling a Tupperware box of left-over spaghetti. He wasn't comfortable, and he snapped at my hands whenever I tried to feed him. So just as we moved from caravan into our much more comfortable house, Snake got a more comfortable home too.

His new box was much bigger. Made of black plastic on three sides, with a sliding door across the entire front. A heat lamp hung in the corner of it like a little sun, and we put in a massive log from the garden for him to lounge on. There was also a bowl of water for him to drink-slash-relax in, as well as his familiar pebble flooring. He seemed happier, but it's hard to read the emotional landscape of snakes. I continued to feed him, and he continued to live in the corner of my room atop a colossal shelf.

In his new home he found a new place to hang out. There was a shallow ridge bordering the space between its walls and roof, and I'd watch, half in amazement, half in horror, as he climbed and slithered up to wedge himself into the ridge, such that his body acted as some sort of decorative skirting board for the top of his home. However, his ability to remain in this spot was tenuous at best, and I remember distinctly the terror I felt as I was pulled from sleep for the first time by the sound of a now three-foot snake crashing from his resting place on the roof down onto his log, and pebbles, and drinking water. I flicked on my bedside lamp, expecting an intruder, only to see Snake splayed around his container like an exposed intestine, as shocked as I was at what had happened. I got the sense that Snake was embarrassed by what happened, his energy felt rosy-cheeked, like when you fall in public and look around to see if anyone has seen. This didn't teach him any lessons, however, as he continued to climb and fall and climb and fall. And I simply got used to it, like anything else.

Snake was about five years old when he died.

I looked up how long they usually live for afterwards. The internet told me that, in the wild they live as long as six to eight years, but in captivity they can live as long as twenty-three years. The oldest on record was thirty-two, a snake that was older than I am now. So, I felt that I had failed him. He didn't even live as long as his wild-counterparts who probably died violent, terrible deaths. Instead, he died quietly in the corner of my bedroom. Maybe if I had loved him more, if I had actually given him a name he would have lived longer. I used to imagine him dying of loneliness, spending the years of his life coiled up in a box, with visitors appearing at his window to stare at him every so often. It was no way to live.

I was outside playing basketball with a friend when he died. It was a warm day. My father appeared again, just as he had when he brought the snake to me in the first place. He was carrying a shovel, and on the shovel was Snake, stiff and lifeless, no longer curled and coiling, but straight like an arrow. I could see the full-length of him now, and how thick he had gotten. He was at least four-feet long, and almost as thick as my wrists—a giant compared to his infant self.

'Your snake died,' he said, lifting the shovel slightly, gesturing for me to look at the dead reptile.

I stopped dribbling the basketball.

'Oh, that's sad,' I replied, saying the thing I thought was most appropriate. My father lingered for a moment.

'It is alright... I'm gonna bury him out the back,' he said, turning back towards the wooden gate he'd appeared through. I watched him leave, almost relieved that Snake was dead, now free from the burden of looking after something I was afraid of.

At the back of our house we had a garden. Beyond the garden was a colossal corn-field. Over the years, when my parents were out, my brother and I would take the opportunity to run around in it, creating haphazard crop-circles, destroying produce in our heedless fun. We didn't understand what we were doing, didn't know the farmer knew our parents, didn't care that our carelessness was costing money, life.

Between our garden and the cornfield there was a border of tall coniferous trees. I've never known what kind of trees they were, but they were huge and green, and their leaves smelt and tasted sour, not broad, brittle leaves, but more like the leaves they give our in churches around Easter. These acted as the barrier between our house and the farmland beyond.

When my father went to bury Snake I assumed he'd use the shovel to dig a shallow grave. Instead, he used the shovel as a make-shift catapult, and as I stood at the top of our drive, planning my next drive to the basket, I watched as my poor, dead snake sailed high into the air, up over our trees, twirling and coiling, briefly alive once again, and hurtling to his final resting place among the stalks of maize, never to be seen again. Most likely to be eaten by wild foxes and rats. It was fitting in a way, a corn snake finding its grave in a corn field.

I rushed to the back garden, alarmed and confused.

'I thought you said you were going to bury him?!' I shouted at my father as I crossed the garden.

He turned, the slightest smirk on his lips.

'Yeah, I did sure. An aerial burial.' Time had moved on. My father and I were both involved in the same basketball club; me as a player, and him as assistant coach and secretary. That made us closer than ever, we had a real thing to bond over as father and son. So maybe Snake sensed he was no longer needed. He was no longer the singular and extremely bizarre thing that tied us together. So maybe that's why he let go, opted out earlier than his slithering counterparts. He sailed over the trees and into the field, his earthly duties completed.

And that was the end of my pet snake.

DEAD MAN'S TAILS

It has come to pass over the last number of years that several pieces of clothing belonging to dead men have fallen into my possession. After funerals, when the time comes to separate out the belongings of those who have died, my name has been uttered in rooms I did not inhabit.

"Daragh will wear that," or "I'll say it to him anyway," and very soon after my wardrobe welcomes a new jacket, or a wool jumper that has already lived a full life with someone who no longer exists in this world.

And it is a strange thing to wear a dead person's clothes. Not strange meaning peculiar, but strange in that their essence is present in a way so long as I continue to wear their jacket or their hat, say. That has a strangeness to it. There's a sense of responsibility to wear their clothes well, with good intentions. Because whenever I do wear their clothes, I think of them for however long, and I remember this and that memory about them, and in this way they live on. Their clothes a practical solution for me, but an extension of their time on this earth, too. So I try to wear them honestly, and on my best days, to pay whatever morsels of respect I can to the men who wore them before me. It's in these small ways that things maintain their importance. This is how we remember loss beyond grief.

An Adidas Sweatshirt

The first piece of clothing I came to possess is a black Adidas sweatshirt with three white-stripes running the length of both arms. It was too big for me when I got it at seventeen. I wear it during winter months, usually on runs but sometimes when the night is very cold in bed.

It belonged to my very best friend, Erbie. He took his own life when he was eighteen and left an unfillable hole in my life, in many people's lives. I also inherited other things from him—dress shirts I'd never wear, shoes that would never fit—but the sweatshirt has stayed and likely will continue to. Each time I pull it from between my hanging clothes I think of him—mostly of the good times spent laughing or playing basketball—and it keeps him alive with me in the most subtle way.

I also wear it when I exercise because exercising was how we spent a lot of our time together. He had an awkward yet effective jump shot. He got angry when, somehow, I beat him one-on-one outside my parents home one Autumn afternoon. I remember that day every time I wear a black Adidas sweatshirt that was too big for me when I inherited it, but fits just fine now.

Liam's Dress Coat

I never knew Liam very well. The few times I did meet him I was a very small child and he felt intimidating. But he was gentle and friendly. He gave me €2 at a time in my life when €2 was the equivalent of enormous riches.

Liam worked as a forester. After he died, his family uncovered a secret he'd kept. In a forest near Killea in Donegal, Liam had a Celtic cross planted using trees that were different to the rest of the woods. It can only be seen from the sky. Liam never got to see it, and I'm almost certain he didn't tell a single soul about it. He wanted it to be discovered.

Liam was my uncle through marriage. He and my aunt and two cousins lived in Donegal and they all had the accents to prove it. But they were originally from Cork. When Liam passed I was given his dress coat, something I would have never thought to buy myself. It's black and has a hood you can zip on and off. I wear it when formality is necessary, or when it is bitter out and extra layers are required.

And each time I do, I am reminded of my cousins in Donegal, and of the €2 he gave me, and of the Celtic Cross he secretly planted among a forest in Donegal that can only be seen from the air.

Paddy's Day Jacket

Paddy was my grandfather. He died in 2021. He was much smaller than me so I was surprised that his jacket fit. But then I found out that Paddy rarely wore it because it was too big on him, and then it all made sense, because my grandfather was a hilarious man, whether he was trying to be or not.

I think that's how I'd describe him, and the best way to remember him. He told jokes but he was also funny in demeanour and expression. Old-fashioned as they come and honourable. As long as I knew him he was a good man. He had the best memory I've ever experienced in person, with an ability to cast his mind back to specific days of his childhood at the age of ninety. And I suppose it was fittingly tragic that he developed Alzheimer's at ninety-one which eventually became too much for life to keep up with. In the months before he passed he wouldn't recognise a single person around him, but he'd sit there, still living in the memories of his childhood near Kinsale.

His day jacket feels like a military garment. And since he spent time in the army in WWII, it was fitting that he owned it. I used to wear it more often, but still each time I spot it on the back of the door, hanging in anticipation, it reminds me of Paddy, of his bizarre memory, and of his love of making people laugh.

Paddy's Ralph Lauren Fleece

Both of the things I got from Paddy were actually given to me when he was still alive. They were just clothes that were too big for him. He got smaller the way people do as they age. He was ninety-four at the end. Whenever I tell people that they always say the same thing: "That's some age". And it was in fairness.

I don't ever remember Paddy getting angry. I'm sure he did, though. What I do remember is all the times he brought me and my brother to playgrounds, or for ice-cream. Or when he'd go along with all the mad shite we'd be doing—pretending to cut his hair with his car keys or making potions in the kitchen. I have all three of his names within my own, and he was also my godfather, so I've always felt connected to Paddy more than to other grandparents. I've been lucky enough to know all four of mine.

If ever I have to speak at something where the dress code is somewhere between business and formal, I do my best to put together clothes that will allow me to wear his fleece. I think people live on the most in subtleties like that.

Finnbar's Aran Jumper

Finnbar was my other grandfather's brother, making him my granduncle via my mother. He was a quiet man. Always so quiet. Before Christy died—his other brother but not my grandfather— they were the highlight of all the grandchildren's Christmas. They'd bring elaborate gifts that were too expensive, and as we got older they filled cards with money, more money than we'd be gifted by anyone else. Generosity was his shtick, if you were to describe him in a single word.

He was the last of four brothers to die. I didn't know him very well at all but my mother was close with him until the very end. I imagine it was strange and difficult for her when he died. In fact, I know it was. He was the last remaining connection she had to her own father, who died when I was fourteen. I don't have any of his clothes but this is mainly because he was almost half my size. Although I think there may be a cap around the place that belonged to him.

The Aran jumper in question is this oversized dark-grey sweatshirt bought in Dunnes. So while it may not be real Aran wool, it gives the impression of it. I'm told Finnbar never wore it himself, either. It's big on me, meaning it would have been colossal on him. And seeing as he was a man who was always immaculately dressed in shirt and trousers and tie, there's no way he'd be caught wearing something that was ill-fitting. He was a gentleman, whereas I am something else entirely.

When Finnbar died, I wrote and gave his eulogy. It felt strange, but I spoke with those who were closest to him—my mother and some of her sisters—and with their help we tried to sum up the man as best we could. Looking back, I'm glad I was able to do that for him. There was never much conversations between us, so it felt like a quiet way to say thanks for everything. He preferred the quiet to the loud, always.

There are hats, scarves, shirts I've never worn, too. Things that are too good to be thrown out and kept for the sake of it that may never be worn again. I'm not sure if they qualify as hand-me-downs. A hand-me-down is typically defined by one person growing out of something, which is then passed down to a smaller family member, isn't it? These clothes, however, weren't grown out of. Some of them were never grown into.

But the men who owned them did grow out of life, leaving behind the parts we can remember. And by wearing the clothes some of their life, their goodness, maybe their honour, will soak into me as well, like spiritual osmosis. And with this, I'll be able to lead a quiet, noble life like many of them did.

Who knows, really. But it is a nice thought.

ANTI-CLIMAX

I'd never even fingered anyone before we met and now I was going to have sex.

Against all odds, I was the first of us to lose my virginity. It felt more like a gain than a loss. Fellas would look at you with new faces, like they only just now began to respect you. I was nervous. She was calm and seemed to know what to do, despite insisting she was also a virgin.

"You need to get condoms."

Her smile was an awkward death. There was little to nothing I would not have done for her. A poison she was, one I voluntarily gulped down. I'd get the condoms, of course. I had never put one on before but I would get them now because they were in need of getting. Where I got them would have to be worked out.

Not a chance I was going into the big Tesco alone, with my big 16 year-old head up on me, asking for condoms like a toddler asking to use the toilet while the piss ran down the leg of his jeans. I knew I needed condoms, but I also knew you could walk into the Sex Health Clinic in town and just ask for them.

They'd say nothing, hand you a small brown paper bag and send you on your way. It felt like going to the dentist or a drug deal, even. We'd often go get them, to have 'just in case', but the things would only ever burn holes in bedside lockers.

While buying condoms in big Tesco was embarrassing, for whatever reason, getting them inside the Clinic was a badge of honour. It made no sense to me, but that's the way it was. Buying them was a non-runner, but getting them for free in town made you a sex God.

The big night was Saturday. Nothing else at all could have mattered. We'd been together for around six months. I was certain I was in love and thus, sex was allowed, and indeed, expected. You did hand stuff to each other until such a time that there was a feeling of love or something love-adjacent, and then you both said you wanted to do sex even though you were both scared and nervous and possibly didn't actually want to. The obvious next step in our serious teenage relationship was to have awkward and terrible sex.

I had all the usual worries. What if I finished too quickly? What if I found out from this whole experience that I was gay? What if she hated it, and therefore me, by proxy.

There were anxieties flowing from my brain like a pipe had ruptured. I entered some utterly chaotic queries into Google over the course of several days. She assured me via text there would be nobody in her house for the entire evening and I told her I had acquired Johnnies with an unexpected sense of pride.

Shifting.*

It started with aul' reliable do-it-for-as-long-as-possible shifting. I could just shift her for ages until the nerves crawling around my stomach disappeared. We began on the couch in a sitting room that smelled like vanilla. After about ten minutes she stopped kissing me and asked if I wanted to go upstairs. I nodded, too nervous to actually conjure words. I hoped she couldn't see my horn, even though, in fairness, it was reasonable to have one. It still felt embarrassing to admit, or even show.

The events which transpired were brief, and admittedly disappointing. From beginning to end, and for both of us. I didn't have a clue. Nobody told me whether it was okay for me to make noise, or where to put my hands. My worst fear—finishing within seconds of beginning—didn't come to fruition. Instead I was so nervous I couldn't finish at all.

With no climactic end, we both decided enough was enough after a few minutes of exertion, both of us rolling over to separate sides of the bed—me exhausted and confused, her confused and unsatisfied.

Being a 16 year-old teenage boy meant I wanted to go at it again, and soon. The floodgates were open, and I was now, in my mind at least, somewhat competent at doing sex. However, because we were both teenagers, finding the time and space was all but impossible. Parents lurked in houses like trolls under bridges. I remember her father being a terrifying and angry man, so I literally did not want to be caught with my pants down in his vicinity.

There's an unspoken bond which emerges between you and the first person you have sex with, especially when you care about one another. There's a sense of belonging which doesn't exist before you awkwardly clamber on top.

This sense of serenity drops dead the moment you're told by your girlfriend that her period is late—really late. All of a sudden, you never want to have sex again for as long as you live.

I got the text from her as I sat in English on a Thursday. I hadn't heard from her since the day before, and I imagined it was because of this realization tearing an anxiety-shaped hole in her mind.

I couldn't make sense of it. I felt I'd been cheated in some way—how was I to be a father when I didn't even get to finish? It didn't seem fair at all.

Was it even possible? I didn't know. I had only very limited knowledge of how these things worked. The 'talk' I got was less about the technical details of sex, and more about scaring me into walking around with a condom on at all times.

But there we were, anyway, despite the scare-mongering, despite the 'advice'; 16 year-old soon-to-be parents, who'd had sex but not enough, I thought, to warrant a baby, a child on the way. Herself was late, and I was in English class.

Being sixteen, almost a man, and having been foolishly gifted with an overwhelming belief that things would always work out for me in the end, I naively figured that, if it came down to it, I could be a teen-father. I could still play basketball and sit my exams, and travel, and be worry-free, and live out my dreams while raising a baby. This conclusion resulted somewhat from privilege (a word that wasn't yet in the public lexicon circa 2011), but mostly it was derived from a brain that was inherently, undoubtedly, entirely stupid.

I was in love. I had engaged undeniably in what one would call sex. I had not been able to finish despite my best efforts. And now, thanks to incredibly bad luck, I was going to father a child.

Everything was going to be fine, I told myself, everything was going to be fine.

*Shifting is an Irish slang-term for kissing. Other synonyms include; meeting, necking, and mauling (and this last one is definitely the worst of the lot).

AFTER PRAGUE

She told me she hated me quite regularly. Then she would kiss me.

Caterina was 20 years old and strong-willed. If there was something she didn't like she said it up front, unapologetically. I think this is why I fell in love with her. Caterina was mature, more mature than me in a lot of ways. Although I was older, she'd done more living—travelling and working in different countries, hopping from place to place at a moment's notice, becoming a citizen of the world. She'd also led a difficult life. She'd experienced so much in such a short amount of time. Her eyes were the colour of knowledge.

She told me that when things were really bad for her before we met, she'd have sex with three or more men a day. She had sex when she was bored or feeling low. She used sex as an attempt to make herself feel better. It made me feel insecure and uncertain about our future. Could I really trust her? Could I really make a relationship work with her.

"You're a sex addict?" I asked, and she said she had been and could be again.

On that first day, I stood outside the door of the apartment we'd booked for the next five nights. It was all excitement and nerves, spiralling around my beating heart. When she opened the door she screamed and hugged me, and kissed me as if to make sure I was real.

I hadn't seen her in three weeks. I was barely able to put down my bags as she kissed me all over. She cooed and whispered "I missed you," and I told her the same. The apartment was small and the only bed was a fold-out couch. But we hardly clocked it. Sex with Caterina was like nothing I'd ever experienced. It felt guilt free for the first time in my life. There was no fear of judgement. No sense of shame—Shame couldn't reach me all the way from Ireland.

Despite the insecurities, I knew I loved Caterina after that first night in Prague. I didn't tell her right away. It seemed too soon and too bizarre to love someone so fully. It didn't make sense that I could feel so strongly after such little time. I told myself I was just getting caught up in the romance of something I'd never felt before. Emotions—all kinds of them—were full and vibrant for the first time, rather than far away and numb.

Caterina had been to Prague several times. She'd been travelling for over two years. Her family were wealthy but broken. She showed me pictures of them—of her brothers and mother and father—and it was clear she had love for her brothers but had a complicated relationship with her parents. She hadn't seen her parents since she'd left, but she'd seen her brothers many times. I showed her pictures of my family too, but my relationships weren't as complicated as hers appeared to be.

"Your brother is much better looking than you," she joked, and kissed my neck.

Caterina wanted to study architecture and often pointed out features of building I would have never noticed. She adored the Charles Bridge. She blurted out unrehearsed facts—things she found interesting, dates, measurements, styles—details no tour guide would ever care to mention. She loved to use the word 'typical'. English wasn't her first language and she used this word as an anchor, squeezing it into places it didn't belong.

"This is a typical example of the gothic style of architecture."

It was a beautiful, crisp November morning as we walked the bridge. We laughed and pointed out statues and views as we meandered along. Caterina kept calling it the Carl Bridge, losing some letters in translation.

She was all I could focus on. She was all I wanted to focus on. There was so much life in her that looked nothing like mine. The way I felt around her was the way I always hoped I could feel, it felt like I was alive.

We continued up the hill to Prague's medieval castle and we looked out over the city. Red roofs, sparkling water, the bluest sky. The sun held court above us on its own; there wasn't a single cloud. But the sun still had winter's weakness; we could still see our words condensing as they left our mouths. Inside the castle grounds we drank hot wine which tasted like ketchup. We wandered about with no real aim, talking about everything and nothing. Caterina didn't like to drink as much as me, and she smoked if ever she did get drunk. She mentioned she wanted to settle down somewhere eventually but she wasn't sure where that might be.

"I'd like to visit Ireland, maybe. Not for you obviously, but maybe it will suit me better." She stuck her tongue out at me. I smiled and held her gaze.

When we returned to the old town we ate gelato despite the cold. Caterina insisted.

"The gelato in Venice is much-a-better."

She exaggerated her accent and shook her pinched fingertips at me. I couldn't argue. She was very certain of this fact.

We walked the entirety of Prague hand in hand that day, absorbed by one another. I found myself doing the things I usually despised to see happy couples doing when I was single—holding hands, kissing, and staring at each other. Over dinner we talked about the future and how uncertain it was for us. She feared she'd never see me again if I returned to Ireland.

"It'll work if we want it to work."

And I did want it to work. I think she just needed to hear it from me. She needed reassurance. In the same conversation, Caterina brought up Switzerland again. Most men treated her terribly when she worked there during the summers.

"All they want is to fuck me and then they leave. That's it."

She was so matter-of-fact about it.

"And any man I've been in a relationship with, no one has ever even bought me flowers. I've never been given flowers."

She said she'd be returning to Switzerland again to work the following summer.

"Why would you go back to a place where you're treated so badly?" I was trying to understand.

She shrugged, "The money is good."

When we got back our apartment that evening, I told her I had to call my mother and would follow her up in a bit. She was suspicious, and later she told me she thought I was calling another girl behind her back. It was late. I ran through narrow streets to the only flower shop that was still open. I picked up a bit of everything; daisies and roses and tulips and lilies. The cashier wrapped my selection with paper while she chatted on her phone, securing the brown paper with cello tape.

I was sweaty and out of breath in the doorway when I arrived back. Caterina started crying when I revealed the flowers. She took them in one hand and held my chin in the other.

"Thank you." Her eyes were bright with tears.

We had sex, and then I showed her a poem I'd written for her, and she told me she loved me for the first time. It felt all perfectly clichéd and Hollywood, the way love was always portrayed. And of course I told her I loved her back. Even though I hadn't known her a month previous. We made plans to meet again in Venice in December. I was going there anyway towards the end of my trip, so we planned to spend ten days exploring the north of Italy together. She said we could go to the beach in the town where she came from if it wasn't snowing. Then we'd visit Venice and Verona and Milan before I flew home. I felt our lives slotting together.

Prague was a fever dream. None of it felt real. And maybe none of it was real. Maybe we were both caught in the moment precisely because it lacked reality. It was the romance you only see people experience on holidays, or in rom-coms. Even when we did simple things, like grocery shopping, it felt more vibrant with her than it ever did back home. Being away, being free, and being with her, drew life out of the even most mundane things.

Caterina cooked for me. Pasta that was simple and Italian and wonderful. The morning after we visited the Kafka museum, and we sat at the square overlooking the clock tower drinking beer at lunchtime. She helped me pick out a scarf to bring home to my mother in a Christmas market, something silk with blooming hues of gold and blue. We ate goulash. We petted dogs and we talked to strangers in an Irish bar. She kissed me whenever she got the urge and she'd always insist on coiling her fingers between mine. I was feeling affection I wasn't used to. My heart was warm with her. She was a drug to which I was addicted, and I knew she felt the same way.

Yet under all of it there was mistrust and there was deceit. I didn't really believe that she hadn't been with another person while we were apart. I didn't even truly mind if she had been with others, I just didn't want to know about it. Then there was deceit on my part, because I had been with someone else. I didn't want to know if she was sleeping with others, and so I assumed to return the favour. We were both single, travelling through Europe separately. We both avoided talking about commitment. We'd said we loved each other, but people who love one another don't do this. They don't keep secrets and they don't look elsewhere for love. We loved one another, or so we said, but I had slept with someone else, and I would again. I knew I should have felt some remorse for this. I knew I should have, but I couldn't feel it.

Our final two days were spent in an echo-chambered bliss, the rest of the world faded out of view. And yet, on some level I knew that what we had wasn't real. It felt superficial, fragile, insecure. Neither of us trusted the other fully. Caterina would makes jokes about sleeping with other men whilst also saying she could never share me with anyone else. There were subtle cues, slight choices, that highlighted our faulty foundation. We never used each other's phones, for example, or I wouldn't let Caterina read my notebooks. Things you'd easily miss, or choose to ignore. Warning signs that what we had might be different to what we thought we had.

After Prague Caterina planned to go to Germany to visit her best friend and work on a farm. She never stayed anywhere for too long. She'd stay there for a week or two before heading home to Italy for a few weeks, and then she'd move on again.

"Why don't you come to Hungary with me?" I asked her.

"Because I'm going to Germany."

"Do you have to go there?"

"Well, do you have to go to Budapest?"

After that, we dropped it. We'd be going our separate ways.

The city was frostbitten on our way to the station. Patches of shiny white still endured where the morning sun hadn't yet reached. We didn't speak much then, silenced by the uncertainty of our future together. I gave Caterina my tan Patagonia cap to keep safe until we met in Italy. I didn't want her to give it back. It was my way of showing her that we'd definitely see one another again. We weren't really certain of where or when we'd see one another. We just hoped we would.

I got on the train just before it began to pull out of the station. Caterina idled on the platform before turning back, my cap resting on her head, and made her way to a train that would take her in the opposite direction of me.

AN ESSAY ON ADHD

ADHD isn't something I ever suspected having. I didn't imagine that it lurked in my mind. That my brain was an ADHD brain. But it is. I know that now. Which means that my brain has always been this way. Nothing has changed. I've just gained additional knowledge.

I didn't show symptoms as a child. There are several reasons for this. My life had constant structure—go to school, to my grandmother's, go to training, do your homework, go home. I didn't experience symptoms because my life was organised for me.

I wasn't the type of child that acted out in class. I wasn't running around classrooms or disruptive. I was diligent, curious, quiet. Sometimes symptoms don't start until later in life. This is true for me. They began to take shape when my life began to lose shape. When I started needing to structure my own life, ADHD started to wake up.

I also had something called Adolescent Photographic Memory. I could easily recall anything I'd read and understood from the age of eleven, right up until I was around twenty-three. Which made school relatively unchallenging. Aside from subjects where memory wasn't the biggest advantage—Maths and Languages—I found tests, homework, exercises dull but not difficult.

So maybe this is why ADHD didn't affect me as a child. Because

I didn't need to focus as much as others to remember things.

I became an adult who had ADHD but didn't know about it. My ability to attend was wrote off as disinterest, boredom, apathy. I jumped in and out of relationships, constantly fascinated by the next shiny thing.

I am a magpie. I have always been a magpie.

When I get the diagnosis it is accidental. It is a work opportunity. It is a content collaboration situation. I do the consultation so I can make a video about what a consultation looks like. So I do not expect it when the psychologist tells me I should proceed with a diagnostic assessment. My world changes and remains exactly the same after she utters a sentence she's spoken hundreds of times.

A month passes and after this month passes I have my official diagnosis. Black and white and obvious. When I tell my mother she isn't surprised. I wonder about this. If it's not surprising then why was I never taken to be assessed before. The symptoms weren't showing as a child. I need to remind myself of this. She couldn't have known.

The symptoms emerged in my twenties. When I started working for myself. When I started writing. When I had to begin organising my own life. Focus is here but is ever-moving. Chasing something until another anything comes along to chase. I feel sorry for my brain because it must be exhausted.

I continue to be dysfunctional in relationships. I have new knowledge but it hasn't yet integrated. I am still fighting against an urge to run. But now I know this urge to run is actually my brain's desire for stimulation.

Being called a fuckboy for having a brain that doesn't work the same as other brains is a thing that happens. People don't understand but I don't think they're trying to. There's something human about that. Dark but human. I understand their lack of desire to understand.

I have to tap my leg when my brain is overstimulated. When it feels like my heart might explode from all the information running through my mind. I tap my left leg with two fingers, find a rhythm that will slow down my brain. Find a rhythm that feels less intense. Just find a rhythm because I'm out of one.

It's easy to do and people don't usually notice. And if they do notice they never say. Sometimes I fall asleep to this tapping. Pushing my mind away from the noise and into the pattern of sleep so I can drift off. Some days I wake up and my teeth are sore or there's a fresh cut on my bottom lip. I wonder if my body was fighting my mind again, making sure it stayed turned off so I could rest.

I am constantly engrossed in decision paralysis. I can never get anything done because I'm trying to do so many things all at once. Like trying to force too many objects through a single funnel. Everything gets stuck. I do what I can to be productive but the idea of being productive is based on brain conditions that are not present inside my skull. Productivity for me looks entirely different. To people obsessed with money and corporations it looks unproductive. I am productively unproductive. Every day ends with feeling like I haven't done enough.

Here's another example: I thought of another point to make while writing the last paragraph and have already forgotten what that point was.

It is rare that my brain is quiet. There are so many things to focus on. My brain finds them all and oscillates between them at a pace I can't keep up with. My focus ricochets around the place, honing in on something briefly before moving onto the next and then the next and then the next. If people who don't experience this could experience it for even an hour, they'd be amazed that I can get anything done at all.

It's not all bad. I have so many ideas. Most of them are shite but the sheer quantity of them means that I often have a good idea. If I can remember it long enough to write it down then the good ideas blossom. Last night I had a dream full of good ideas. ADHD doesn't sleep. These ideas pertained to why I'm feeling off lately— the dream told me that I'm homesick, that I sometimes feel left out by the poetry community, that I need to be a better person.

If people aren't right in front of me I forget they exist. Not exist, but their presence is necessary for me to think about them. If you don't know I have ADHD this can seem self-absorbed. But it's not like that. I spend most of my time worrying about the thoughts of the people who are currently present. So if you're not here you're just not on the list. Which makes it hard for me to do anything long-distance, or keep up with friends and family. It all feels so overwhelming. It feels like I'm letting everyone down.

I have ADHD. I am not it, though. It's just a way to describe how my brain works. It is not my identity, nor my personality. But it affects these things. It contributes. Parts of me that my friends and family love about me wouldn't be there without it. Some of my flaws wouldn't exist without it either. It's just a thing. It's how my brain is wired. How it works and doesn't work. I'm not keen to be defined by it. This feels too reductive, too simplistic to say that I am who I am because of these symptoms. Do we define rivers by the ways they bend?

When people find out, even ones who have known me my whole life, they treat me differently at first. Like I am wounded or fragile or broken. But this isn't the case. I've been like this my whole life, and will continue to be for the rest of it.

Slow is smooth and smooth is fast. I met an Australian stuntman once who told me this. He had ADHD, too. I didn't understand it when he said it in 2021. But I get it now. For my brain to work I need to slow the pace, let it rest, take one thing at a time. We're just out here taking it one thing at a time.

YOU KNOW IT WHEN YOU FEEL IT

We elected to play table tennis.

Months had passed since I last saw them. Them; the wonderfully Italian woman and incredulously optimistic man from Cork. We met in Milan months before and now we were here, they drinking Murphy's and me drinking water like the temporary dullard I had to be. A friendship magic'd out of thin air. In the grand calculus of the universe, it was all so incredibly unlikely. They'd fallen in love, God bless them, on the road before we'd met. And now we were what you'd call good friends. Not seeing each other often but making time when we could. You can't predict the road, nor who will walk along it beside you.

Other memories from travelling are not so fond. Other friendships did not persevere. Tenuous social media connections are all that remain. Not every destination can be a highlight real. Not every trip lives up to expectations. The bar is set so high, how could every place on Earth succeed in meeting?

Berlin, for example. Perhaps it's because I lost a love there. Or maybe it's because every other day in Berlin is spent hungover or worse. Whatever the case, the capital city of Germany strikes an unsettled chord within me.

London, a place I hope to one day live for at least a little while, strikes me directly in this way like sunlight through the curtains.

Sadness sits in the stomach, yesterday's optimism drowning. I could never put my finger on why exactly this is. Until we played table tennis in Cork while I drank an embarrassing pint of water. It sort of just emerged from the ether.

It's the uncanny valley. Sort of.

London reminds me of home in that everyone speaks in the same way, and more or less has the same sense of humour, and diversity of values and all the rest. Nothing feels alien, the way things do in Spain or France, with foreign words stupidly falling out of my incapable mouth. London feels like home in all the ways aside from the ones that are necessary.

Home, in its essence, is a sense of belonging. It runs deeper than familiarity. Have you ever returned to a childhood home where a new family now lives? Familiar, but you don't belonging there. It's no longer home. Just a house you used to live in.

London for me causes this uncanny valley flavoured melancholy. It feels like home but I am alone there, without belonging, and thus it is not home. There is no love, no tribe, no sense of adhesion. It's the veneer of home without the feel of it. Artificial. Like swimming in a pool rather than the ocean, there's something indescribable missing. Walking around London produces a sense of unease, and —until recently—unplaceable nausea. It's as if my very atoms are screaming for home, thinking it exists in London, and finding that there is no semblance of it to be found.

The ghost of belonging is all I find there. Something so very close that I might easily tolerate it for years without really noticing it. Until I return home. And my shoulders relax. And harmony washes over my soul. It's in these small inexplicable subtleties. A range of tiny nothings that compile into everything.

You can't really describe home, but you know it when you feel it.

I delivered this sermon of sorts to Italy and Cork, a pint of water in one hand, a worn table tennis paddle in the other, and I remarked that I should attempt to write it down.

So I did, and now I have.

ARE YOU READY?

" Are you ready?"

The short sentence appears blankly on my screen. I reply, 'Yes.' It becomes clear later that I am wrong about this.

The pictures sent back aren't the ones I'm ready for. Rather than seeing the promised nude images of her, this woman I am courting through the internet, they are nude images of myself. Taken through a mirror, phone slightly obscuring my face but not enough to plausibly deny. These images are of me, pictures I had taken in the silent valleys of loneliness and desperation.

'You have ten seconds to tell me to stop or I will send these to all your family on Facebook.'

It's interesting, this three-word question precedes a litany of both good and bad things. Dates, races, births, flights, exams, surgeries, parties, weddings, funerals, bedtimes, stage times, fights. The asking of such a question implies an assumption that the asked may not be ready. It infers urgency—hurry up, get ready if you're not already, why on earth are you not ready yet?

A question that bookends some of our most life-changing moments. The question elicits tightness, tension. We brace for impact, we ready ourselves.

When she typed this message to me, she essentially a stranger, I felt fear. The type of fear that is good and cold, winter grass frost-tipped with excitement. When the right person asks you this question, you feel alive. Emboldened and terror-struck, at once, together.

I tell her that I am ready, not understanding just yet the significance of this question.

My inappropriate readiness is now unavoidable. Was I ready? Certainly not. Rather than being satisfied in my appropriate preparation, I am now reeling, panic exploding and racing through my veins. The world closes in. I cannot think. I cannot think.

Blood behaves strangely when we feel we're in danger, rushing like ambulances to the areas deemed most needing. Faces flush red, ears tingle, brain is at maximum capacity, heart attempting to flap its wings hard enough so as to exit the body. Panic is terrific. And I mean that literally. It is tremendous, engulfing, insurmountable in its intensity. It is neither good nor bad, but rather, both. All of it all at once, swirling, swarming like a great number of bats exposed to light. Panic is the system becoming over stimulated. Panic is when the system has failed to prepare, to become ready. Panic is what occurs as my own nude images are sent back to me with insidious intent.

The air is sucked out of the room, seemingly through my phone. And then she begins The countdown.

'10.'

'9.'

'8.'

'7.'

I do what any sane person would do. I tell her/them/whoever this is, to stop.

Then nothing, briefly.

Then my phone begins to vibrate. This girl, who I'd met on a dating app, who is now threatening to send my images to my family, is ringing me.

I answer.

'Hello?'

'You are going to send me €2000 or I will send these pictures.'

The voice isn't a Cork woman's voice. It is a man's voice, accented but unplaceable. My face feels drained of anything worth living for as this reality, this deceit, sets in. I feel violated, like someone has reached inside me without permission.

'Why are you doing this? Who are you?'

'It doesn't matter. You have it real nice in Ireland with your money and your nice jobs. It's not like that in Nigeria. I want some of that money.'

'Why are you making that my fault? I don't have that kind of money.'

'Sure you do, I can see from LinkedIn you have a good job.'

A further intrusion. Each sentence feels as if this person is illegally inside me.

'I don't have that kind of money.'

'What can you afford?'

'Five hundred euro.'

'No, that is not enough. Do you have Bitcoin?'

'No.'

'How don't you have Bitcoin?'

'I just don't.'

'Okay, you will have to get some and—listen to me—you will have to download this app.'

This is when I hang up the first time. The phone rings again immediately.

'Why did you hang up on me?'

'I thought you told me to?'

'No. Now, you will have to download this ap-'

'Honestly man, fuck off. Send them for all I care.'

I hang up again. I block him. I am terrified.

When threatened, our sense of consciousness collapses to the fundamental self. At full capacity, when we are safe, fulfilled, actualised, our consciousness burst the banks of self-centredness. Our sense of self disperses into the lives of other people, we care less about protecting 'I' and more about enriching 'We'. But, when threatened, we invert this. Our level of consciousness contracts. I can feel this happening—the world collapses inward, only able to think of how the current situation will affect me. All that is important is self-preservation. And in this moment, this pitiful moment of imminent mortification, all I can concern myself with is how to wriggle free from the grips of what is unfolding. I would,

I think, have paid the money if I could afford to. Five hundred was something I could have paid, and in this initial moment of deep-rooted fear and panic I would have done so had this intruder accepted it.

Initial, intense panic subsides. It cannot sustain itself. Explosions don't go on for eternity with limited fuel. There is the initial violence and then there is the slow, inevitable decay. By the time my intruder messages again—this time on Instagram—reducing his price to accept my five hundred euro counter offer, I know, somehow, that paying him anything would be a bigger mistake than sending pictures to a stranger in the first place. Because once a scammer like him has someone like me on the hook, he'd keep returning to the well, drying out my accounts under the threat of exposure, and each time I'd pay a little more and a little more, accepting the sunk cost of giving in to blackmail.

An hour or so after these interactions, it appears that this twisted serpent has slinked off, no doubt to wreak the same havoc on some other unsuspecting and lonely man, using the images of a young woman who had no doubt also been swindled to do so. My pictures are no longer mine. Stolen. My vulnerability weaponised.

I am angry—at myself for having been so naïve, at this monster for taking my most intimate self and using it against me, at the world for it being a place where this could happen at all. I don't have control of anything and I crave it, I need it. So, rather than waiting for this evil of the internet to seep into my life in the night, I tell the world. I type out the words. I press send. I take what little control I have and I use it.

'I'm currently being blackmailed by someone who has naked images of me and is asking me for €2000 in order to prevent them being posted, which I'm obviously not gonna do. So if you see images of me somewhere, enjoy them I can guess!'

Virality works best online for tragedy. If you have bad news, something terrible, people will listen. We, sadly, feed on it. It gives us life. It gives us a reference point for gratitude. At least that's not happening to me, we think. And so as the hours pass into days I find myself becoming an unwilling example of intimate-image sexual abuse—something I thought I was too privileged to ever become a victim of. Radio stations call, as do newspaper journalists, many of them kind, some of them treating me as nothing more than a commodity to be used for ratings. 'It'll be great!" They say, completely oblivious to emotional thin-ice I find myself on. Each hour passing bringing forth new and unpredictable waves of anger, remorse, contempt. By Thursday—three days after the incident—I am strung out, viscerally aware of the familiar tendrils of depression trying to take hold at the frail edges of my reduced mind.

My phone is alive, excited even. Message after message. Phone calls from strange numbers are now dread-inducing. Every message from a person I do not know carries with it the potential for further attacks. Most of these messages are from well-meaning, kind-hearted people, reaching out beyond themselves to help. To soothe. To make sure I know that I am safe, that I am loved. But I cannot feel it. My brain is not in the position to absorb it. I am locked into survival mode. Everything feels like it could be a threat. Everything feels laced with violence.

We are at our best when our consciousness is expanding, delving beyond our own borders. We are un-depressed, un-self-involved. We are serving others. Many of the people reaching out are examples of this higher-consciousness. In these days after the intrusion, I am not this. I am so far in distance from this that I do not remember how it feels. I am shrunken, a shadow, reduced to hyperfocus on the self, unable to focus on anything beyond what is threatening me.

And it is this, in truth, that is the biggest violation. This reduction. Made to feel so small, forced to be so small. Diminished to the version of human that can only focus on survival. This is the violation. No longer a human-being. Forced to regress to an animal that has been cornered.

Time doesn't care. It trundles on regardless. Slowly, I subside with it. As weeks and then months and then a year passes, the fear and panic recedes like a waveless tide. There is no clear line that marks where this experience changes from immediate panic to unpleasant memory. At some point the tide is more out than in, and I am more at peace than distressed. I learn to live with this violation, absorb it into the history of my life. The tide has gone out, and I am left lying on this desolate beach, beginning to breathe again, gazing up at a velvet blue sky I am still grateful to look up at.

SPITEFUL PRICK

The carpeted floor of the front room of my parent's house was a treat for the bare soles of my feet. It was an ambiguous summer's day; one that had seen sun and rain and cloud all in the same afternoon. The heat had maintained its hold on the air, which clung to clothes like damp breath. There was a deadness to it that had the effect of suffocating the sound of silence. The windows were open on the north and east facing walls which were made-up primarily of glass planes, causing the room to become a sun-trap during the mornings. Now, however, in the shade of the afternoon, it was the coolest room in the house, and was a much coveted oasis away from the heat of the outside world.

I took to the couch, which was a soft and needed resting place decorated with more cushions than one could possibly ever require. The relentless sun and garden work had taken a toll on me, and I felt the nap which I had planned for the next hour had been well and truly earned. As I landed down on the grey cushioning, I could feel a slight breeze flow in from the open windows and I could hear birds chirping what sounded like a happy conversation outside. There was energy on the air that is only felt on certain days during the Irish summer. In the distance someone was cutting lawn, and if I listened even further I could hear the sounds of cars driving away; it was a carefree sort of day in the sun.

Of course the air was also alive with the playful sounds of flying insects. The ability of flies, bees and wasps to seek out and find an open window in the summer months is something that will never cease to amaze me. Further to that, their inability to rediscover said window once they go through it is something that will never cease to confuse me.

Nestling into a slumber was interrupted abrasively by a familiar buzzing against the glass. A clear sign of a flying insect that had gotten itself inside but was now struggling to exit. My mind bounced randomly to how this was a nice metaphor for how we'd gotten into a situation with climate change; unable to get our way out of a situation we created. I noted to write that down later, knowing full well that I'd forget. Then the reverb of the glass disappeared and I could hear the buzzing out in the vast isolation of my parents' front room. The buzzing was too crisp and sharp to be a housefly. The buzz had too much purpose and didn't sound as erratic as the flight pattern of a fly. The buzzing was also too urgent and pointed like the prick of a needle to be any sort of bee. They usually lazed along, often fat with pollen and not in any hurry. That only left us with one other option, the only option which would have me open my eyes and peer around to ensure my safety; there was a bastard wasp in the room.

I flicked my eyes around the place as I sat up to find the buzzing aggressor. My weariness of wasps was well rooted in my childhood, having been stung between the fingers on the pier of the seaside town of Ardmore as a boy. Ever since then, I had been actively at war with the no-good wannabe pollinators. They had been sent from the future to cause havoc and evoke panic anywhere they'd go, of that I was certain.

This particular wasp had found its way toward the ceiling, which at a cursory glance, may seem harmless. But it wasn't harmless. It knew I was there and it circled around the centre light, planning its next move. I was on my feet in an instant, and had already picked up a book from the bookcase nearby, a heavy encyclopaedia for the letter L. I was just then making peace with the fact that I was about to take this wasp's life. Although I never liked taking the life of my aerial visitors, in this moment I knew it was either it or me. In one smooth motion I swung the book at the wasp as it turned an invisible corner in my direction. A direct hit catapulted the bastard towards the TV stand where it fell quietly to a motionless position on the cream carpet below.

I approached my fallen foe to be doubly sure that it had died. Upon seeing its twitching body, with the legs slightly curled, I felt comfortable that I had won this particular battle. I left the body where it fell so that it could act as warning to any other would-be foes to steer clear of this battleground. I also just couldn't have been bothered disposing of the insect's carcass if I'm being completely honest.

I fell back towards the couch. The quick interaction had my heart beating an up-tempo rhythm and I knew it might take me slightly longer than anticipated to drift off into a light sleep. Nevertheless, I was happy to be switching off in a wasp-free environment. The couch was only a two-seater, meaning it wasn't long enough for my six feet and two inch long body, so I curled my left leg in on itself, whilst keeping my right foot planted on the floor. It was a comfortable position, and one I'd fallen asleep in before, so I wasn't bothered by the lack of space to stretch out in.

Soon after, I drifted along the edge of sleep, in a half-conscious delirium. The dreamscape of my fantasies bordered reality, and although I could still feel the room around me, and the carpet underfoot and the air flowing from the window, my mind was already bleeding into a surreal new universe deep within my psyche. This lucid in-between realm was one of my favourite places in human existence.

I was jolted back from the brink of sleep by a loud pain erupting from my right foot. At first I wasn't sure if were part of the dream or part of the room. The pain was intense and pointed and felt as though my foot would explode if it didn't cease soon.

I was miles away now from my half slumber. The oncoming dreamscapes dissipated as the pain took over my occipital and frontal lobes. I looked down past the edge of the couch to see what had brought such suffering to my foot.

The bastard wasp that I'd thought dead was squirming in agony next to my big toe. Having used its stinger, it would certainly die now. After being plucked from the sky by my book wielding hand, the wasp had lost consciousness and appeared to be dying to the untrained and inattentive. When it woke up on the carpet by the TV, with fatal injuries to its wings, rendering it unable to fly, it vowed revenge before it left this earthly plain.

In the ten minutes that followed, as I fell into sleep, the wasp traversed the carpeted plains of my parent's front room, toiling away with its tiny legs along the rough terrain. Oh, the things it must have seen! It then found my bare foot and injected its biting sting between my big and second toes. Although it surely knew it would die if it used its sting, it still wanted me to know that it had won the day.

As I looked down at the dying wasp, squirming from the anguish of having its insides ripped from within itself, while my own foot throbbed from the pain caused by this wasp's last and final act upon the stage of our world, I found a moment within me to respect this malicious insect. It may have been a bastard, but the level of hard-headed stubbornness it had just portrayed was remarkable, and I knew I'd always remember this spiteful prick.

OSMOSIS

I learned about osmosis in school quite some time ago. The way water moves between cells on instinct. The instinct of what, I'm not sure. Osmosis is where water moves through a semi-permeable membrane from an area that has a lot of water to an area that does not.

In a sense the cells become aware of one another, and share around the water so that no cell falls into dehydration. I'm not a scientist. But this is how osmosis seems to be. The cells help each other out. Automatically. It's in their nature.

For a while I think I believed I could fix myself in the same way. Via osmosis.

I thought that if I could lead others to heal, by talking about mental health and writing about it and making people feel that they weren't alone then maybe I'd heal, too. I thought that if I could become a resource for others that their newfound wellbeing would also bleed into me. Their healing might transfer to me via osmosis and we'd all improve together, the way the cells of plants do. That's what I think I must of thought, but it isn't how these things work.

It doesn't work because when those you've helped have adjusted and moved on, and you're left in the silence of their departure, you can still feel it. The pain. You can hear the quiet voices in the blanket of nothing. The unaddressed issues beating in the darkness.

It is of course nice to want to help people. We should all strive to do that as much as we can. However, it is destructive to run from your own issues, and use helping others as an excuse to not have to address them. Despite the enduring hope, there is nobody coming to save us. No one descends from the clouds and makes everything all right.

The only person who can save you is you. A realisation that often comes too late, or not at all.

But we often do have this knowledge, despite pretending not to. We bury it. We know there are things, painful things, which we leave to fester in the darkness like rotting carcasses. We choose to leave them there because we can tolerate them when they are out of sight. Their presence doesn't dwindle, but our awareness of them does. Whatever problems these painful experiences drum up, we learn to endure. We can withstand the pain for the most part.

Until eventually we look back. And we see how much destruction those unresolved issues have caused. We may not realise that we've cut off our own limbs while accepting them to be tolerable sacrifices.

Addressing the unaddressed is painful. And it takes work. So much work that we often opt for the slow destruction of tolerated pain rather than facing up to the monsters. They can seem insurmountable when you look at them all at once. If we ignore them, at least we don't have to look upon the flaws that scar our souls.

No matter what we do, those flaws and ignored faults surface. The cracks appear. Ripples across our personalities. Biting and jagged edges. So it is better, surely, to choose to look upon them now, while you have the strength, and find a way to challenge them head on.

Healing through osmosis doesn't work. We don't have membranes that mental health can seep through from others. Throwing yourself into work doesn't make the problems disappear. Chasing achievement after achievement doesn't erase the pain. I've tried all of these things and none of them work. They just mask the problem. They treat the symptoms rather than the root of the disease. Short-term fixes is all they are, to distract your mind from the fact that there are flaws that need your attention.

We are not yet capable of healing each other through some sort of shared telepathy. Plants can do this. We however, can help one another along. Words are our source, our sole but powerful source. We can communicate and express our emotions. We can reach across the divide like no other creature can, and we can let one another know that we are together. We are one in the same and we will get through whatever needs getting through.

Perhaps this is our osmosis. Our ability to use words. Delicately. Imperfectly. Perhaps this is how we help one another to heal.

TRIPPY-TRIPPY TRIP-TRIP

He stumbled over the rocks, clambering towards us, a plastic cup filled with vodka in his left hand, the other hand working to steady himself, a lit rollie hanging from a drying bottom lip. His smile was drunk and wet, his eyes not focused on our world, his arms descending from sunburned shoulders.

This short hill, a 3-foot incline of man-placed rocks separating our part of the campsite from his, was this young man's Everest. His legs wouldn't obey his mind's intention. He made progress, but then his next footing would be a misstep and he'd find himself once again at the bottom of the short slope, cursing his useless legs, looking up at us, pure helplessness embodied.

We sat there watching in a sort of grimaced laughter, unsure of what to make of his attempt to join us. Wondering what he planned to do once successfully up the rocky hill. Hoping he'd never make it. He had not been invited to join us, nor had we ever spoken to him in the few days we'd been camped there.

His eyes pleaded at us to get rid of the hill that kept him from us. As if we could take away the rocks and make it easier for him to ascend. Not one of us moved to help him, and after several minutes of watching, we all turned back to our conversation and the music emanating from Eoin's portable speaker. Eventually we heard him shout what he'd been shouting all week, his catchphrase, as if he was a Pokémon and this was all he could say.

"TRIPPY-TRIPPY TRIP-TRIP!" he blared, before giving up and collapsing into a nearby tent. It was unclear whether it was actually his own.

We were never given a name so his catchphrase became his unofficial title. Trippy-Trippy Trip-Trip was on the periphery of our experience for most of the music festival, heard screaming in the distance, or stumbling around, never sober, and always after consuming too much of whatever drug he was taking. At one stage he emerged from a half-assembled tent with a clearly infected, new ear piercing, a detail his equally intoxicated friends seemed unbothered by. They were the type of people you knew instinctively to avoid. It rose up the hill from them, a psychic stench, a warning to keep to yourself as much as possible.

"TRIPPY-TRIPPY TRIP-TRIP!"

A call to announce peak intoxication. I didn't speak a single sentence to him, but he became unforgettable. A myth. A fable. As the months passed, far beyond the week-long festival in the south of Spain, his features were still embedded in my mind. The pig-like snout, two lazy eyes with big rings beneath them, ears that stuck out, sore thumbs on either side of his red cheeks. An overbite, hair bleached horribly blonde. A pale body scorched crimson. Whenever I became too drunk from then on, I'd use this phrase—his phrase—as an ode to the party troll of Benicassim, a sign of respect to a man lost in the chaos. Whenever people asked me how the festival went, tales of Trippy were sure to follow. He was the ultimate enigma.

A year passed. Trippy-Trippy Trip-Trip faded into memory.

His hallucinogenic aura became lost in the entropy of the universe. I went to the festival again the following year—the same campsite but with different people. We spent the week with men from Glasgow and women from Kent. We drank heavily and swam in the ocean and stayed up all night listening to music. I don't remember much but I remember being happy. I remember smoking weed on the beach and tumbling in the warm ocean at night.

It was the Friday afternoon, I think. We'd been there since Monday. Live music started on the Thursday, and there we were on the Friday, our fourth day in a row of heavy drinking. Our part of the campsite had become the focal point for good craic, somehow, for whatever reason. Broken tents, and smashed camping chairs, crushed cans and cups littered the flattened grass all around. Pure hedonistic ignorance. It was glorious for all but the environment.

Around our camp, young men and women flocked to pitch camping chairs and drink like fish. Among them was a chap with a surprising ego. There was no shame at all in him. Maybe it was the drink coursing through him. Or the dehydration. Either way, he had the confidence of an armada.

"It's my birthday today."

An answer to an unasked question. Met with uncomfortable

acknowledgments.

"Happy birthday, man" A general response from the crowd gathering to drink. It's always a bit strange when someone demands that you celebrate them.

Minutes passed. Music bumped. Shite talk was shite talked.

"Will I rap for you lot?" Again he chirped up; an unsolicited offer from the birthday boy. It felt more like an FYI than a genuine question. It was met with palpable unease.

Without waiting for a response, he rose from his camping chair to turn down the music pumping from a portable speaker in the middle of the circle. We were all too heat exhausted and drunk to stop him. He was going to rap no matter what happened. This was clearly fated.

He sat back down, cleared his throat, drew in a few essential deep breaths. And then he began to rap, in an English accent not designed for such things.

To this day I don't know what he thought was going to happen. I do not recall the performance, but I know it wasn't at all good. Maybe he thought he'd be discovered, that we'd all sit there in awe of his lyrical prowess, becoming undone by his sheer talent. I suppose if you were confident enough to rap for a group of strangers without any request for you to do so, it would suggest that you have an ego so abnormally sized as to expect the sun and the moon for your efforts.

Instead we all sat there in stunned silence, as he mangled the syllables of a usually somewhat lovely sounding language. We tolerated it. We persevered through the cringey awkwardness as he rapped acapella, first from a sitting position and then rising to a power stance as he got more into his own rhythm. His hands flailing, his eyes fixated on a point just below knee level. It was an unexpected torture. People mostly kept their eyes trained on the ground, afraid to meet his eye. Eyes rose from the ground infrequently to make sure everyone else around was in an equal amount of discomfort. Cursed to endure a concert we couldn't leave and had not consented to. It was the equivalent of a rapper getting onto a Metro train in any of the major European cities, rapping in your face as you commute, and demanding that you pay for the experience.

Eventually he ran out of rhymes. It didn't take long, maybe a minute or so, a minute dragged which on for eternity. He sat back down, his eyes reaching out to us for validation, our eyes avoiding contact at all costs. I looked anywhere but directly at him, sipping from my beer with the hope that I might fall into it.

And this is when I looked over his right shoulder and saw him. A ghost. A spectre. Somehow, against insurmountable odds— Trippy-Trippy Trip-Trip in the flesh. The universe placing he and I there. Of all places, of all people, together again.

It was like being on an alternate timeline. His features were the same, but his demeanour was entirely different. His hair was combed into a trendy sort of comb over. His chest was caved and his shoulders were hunched, reflecting a person who wasn't all that confident. He had no infected earlobes, and his eyes look more aware than I had ever seen them. He sipped quietly from a beer, his body language pleading for no one to pay him attention.

All of a sudden I found myself pointing at him and screaming the name I'd given him. I was tipsy at the least, and so I had no problem calling to him across the throng of mostly drunken men. When he heard it –"TRIPPY-TRIPPY TRIP-TRIP!"—his cheeks darkened, his mind remembering immediately the weight of this phrase, remembering the man he was only a year before. I released a laugh at a joke only he and I understood. No one from the year before was present, or even at the festival. Only he and I knew the truth.

I recounted this man's tale to the crowd, not to embarrass him, but to celebrate his tenacity, his sheer love of the session. As the story went on and lads began to cheer on his prowess, Trippy-Trippy began to relax, becoming enamoured by the encouragement,

When I eventually finished telling them of Trippy's previous festival, how he stumbled from place to place screaming his own nickname, on drugs more often than he wasn't, I lifted my warm can of beer to the sky.

"TRIPPY-TRIPPY TRIP-TRIP!" I hollered.

"TRIPPY-TRIPPY TRIP-TRIP!" the crowd of drunken festival-goers returned, followed by nonsensical screams of hedonistic pleasure as cans were downed and crushed and thrown for a full minute of pure ecstasy.

Soon, the crowd moved their attention onto new stories, and back to the general hum of the music. The rapping birthday boy left, hurt that the attention was no longer on him. Trippy found his way to me, the shy look returning to his eyes. I smiled at him and placed a welcoming palm on his shoulder.

"I was a different person last year, was with a bad crowd, you know?" there were tears in his voice.

"You did no harm to anyone, pal, but it's good to see you doing better all the same." I extended my can to him.

He reached out with his own, the dull metallic clunk of can-on-can was the sound of leaving the past where it belonged. Shortly afterwards, both Trippy-Trippy Trip-Trip and I faded into the drunken Spanish night towards the stage area and I never saw him again.

A FRIDAY AFTERNOON IN BARCELONETA

Men selling mojitos on the beach in mid-October. Tiny Asian women follow minutes later selling massages for a tenner. I sip from a beer I bought at a twenty-four hour shop nearby. I have jeans on. Before I moved here I thought I'd never not be wearing shorts. But this hasn't turned out to be true. Still, the skies are blue and the sun is setting behind us. But it is cold. I can feel that it is cold.

The beach is littered with people and garbage—half buried beer cans and discarded beach paraphernalia. The water is peppered with vague plastics, tinged green and questionable. This beach isn't a first choice. Being the one closest to the city, it's the beach most filled, with tourists, with sellers, with rubbish. But it's the closest one, on the edge of Barceloneta. Normally, in the summer months, we'd make the trek out towards Bogatel, a cleaner, nicer beach that locals tend towards. But we have visitors this weekend who wanted a beach, and we made the decision to come here. It was less work for us, and they'd never know any better. We'd endure the constant pestering for the sake of ease.

They are persistent, the beach-sellers. Incessant. Non-stop like bees collecting nectar. Each time they pass by, they lower their price marginally. Hoping that the new price of three euro might entice us into making a purchase. It doesn't. Mainly because I never carry cash, but also because the idea of buying drinks from a man carrying them around in a plastic bag on the beach feels seedy.

'Beer, Water, Agua, Cerveza!'

I wonder, as this latest punter lingers in comfort despite our discomfort, how much money they make a day. If this line of work is worthwhile. If they sell, say, ten of their drinks a day at six euro a piece, that's a day's wages I suppose. They hardly declare tax on it. Sixty quid to bring home. It doesn't feel like enough to me. Compared to being back home, sixty quid would travel more here. Rent aside, it is cheaper to live here. But maybe the money isn't staying here at all. Perhaps it's being shifted across borders, via the impossible to understand wire to countries where this type of money could make a significant difference.

Where is home for them? What does it look like? This is the thought I'm most wrapped up in as the latest travelling bartender finally gives up and begins towards the next groups of people scattered along the beach like seaweed.

The women selling massages don't have to sell as many to make the same living in theory. But I imagine it's more difficult to flog a massage than it is to sell a cocktail to someone who is already drinking. Definitely more of an upsell. Getting a massage on the beach brings unwanted attention. The spotlight is upon you. Personally, I know already that I could buy a drink but I would never opt in for the public rub down.

"Where do you reckon these lads live?" I ask to no one in

particular. I'm sitting on the sand with my roommate and two of his friends who have come to visit for the weekend. They all three look at me, mostly uninterested.

"What do you mean?" Shay responds with a question of his own.

"Like, do you think they live in apartments like ours? I can't imagine it."

"Yeah, jaysus, I dunno," Shay is scrawling the sand with his fingers, not looking up as he talks.

I decide to drop it. The lads are already focused on the night ahead. The inevitable drunkenness of another Friday night. It's still bright, around 2PM. None of us have had to work today. So we decided to come down to the beach and drink and do nothing. The beach isn't packed but it's busy. Some people are braving the water, even in these cooler temperatures. Not too far down the shore from us, there's a couple staging aesthetic photographs to upload to social media. This type of behaviour depresses me—people doing things just for their Instagram feeds rather than doing things just for the enjoyment of them. I'm aware enough to know this feeling means I'm getting older, slowly growing resentful of how young people behave. It feels nice, in a way, to know I'm aging. Because I can't often feel that I'm growing older. Mostly I still feel the same as I always have, but every now and then I'll have a thought that suggests I'm growing resistant to change, and as such, am beginning to be set in my ways, the years cementing my personality.

I begin to imagine where the Mojito Mongers live. My instinct is that they live in dorms, tens of people cramped into three-bed apartments in places like Raval and El Borne. Living day to day, coming out to this beach and other beaches like it to sell overpriced but convenient cocktails to tourists and expats living in the city. Several families living together, children crying and running around the dark spaces, mothers working together just to get through the long day. How do they spend their evenings, after the day of work is done? Do they spend it like us? Do they drink beers and make dinner and laugh and watch sub-par Netflix shows? It's hard to imagine they do. I imagine them sitting around playing cards in mostly silence. Constant stress, un-leaving worries. And then I wonder am I being a classist prick for not being able relate at all to how they might live their lives.

I barely even look at them when they walk by. I just say, 'No gracias' and hope they won't linger over my shoulder for too long. I'm always aware of the weight of my phone and wallet in my pockets, making sure to keep them concealed. I am making vast assumptions. I am afraid of the city in many ways. And it's most likely this fear that causes the ignorance, that causes my thoughts to assume the worst about people just trying to get by.

We stay on the beach for another hour or so. The punters eventually blend into the background. An unavoidable nuisance, much like the flies and the seagulls. We flick the flies from our skin and we ignore the offer of drinks. One man is selling fresh coconut. He's duped me before, only a few weeks earlier. I was on the beach with a girl when he came over.

"No gracias," I said it before he spoke, the coconut outstretched, pinched between metal thongs. I gauge by his accent and complexion that, like myself, he's not from here. Possibly North African but I can't be certain. He smiles at me, hearing my accent butchering the language.

"Where are you from?" he asked, the piece of coconut suspended between us.

"Ireland," I returned without enthusiasm.

"Oh very cold out there."

"That's true, colder than here anyway."

"For you," he said, waving the coconut in my face.

"I don't have any money, pal,"

"It's okay, take it." He dropped the coconut into my hand and gave another piece to my date. For a moment I saw this as a kindness, but then he didn't leave. The smile left his face. We'd already begun eating the strange fruit.

"Four euro," his demeanour changed entirely, now almost intimidating.

"I told you I don't have any money," I reply, white flesh in my mouth.

"Come on," his hand was outstretched.

The bastard. I rummaged in my pocket and found two 2-euro

coins.

"Here," I stabbed the coins into his open palm.

"No, four euro each." He gave us tiny shards of coconut, one piece each.

"That's all I have on me."

He looked down at the coins and closed his fist. His neck swelled, veins appearing. I sensed violence on his energy. The glare he gave was one brimming with resentment.

"That's all I have, genuinely." This wasn't genuine. I had more, but fuck him. He allowed himself to stare at me a moment longer, attempting intimidation. His brow pointing like an arrow towards the length of his nose. I continued to eat the coconut, feigning disinterest in his attempts to frighten. Eventually he walked away with his winnings, the money he received for giving us free coconut.

When he was a little bit down the beach I looked at my date and said, "What a prick," and she laughed.

And now he's back again as myself and the lads drink beers on the beach. He asks us where we're from and returns the same tired comment about it being cold in Ireland. I warn the lads.

"Don't take it off him, boys, he'll say it's free and then make you pay for it."

He glares at me, annoyed that I've foiled him. I can see his eyes darting all over my face, trying to recognise me. I take a sip from my beer and meet his gaze with a closed smile. He takes his hand back and begins to move on. There are four of us, our average height about six-foot-three, so even though he probably wants to hit me, he doesn't.

The rest of the afternoon bleats on like this. We four drinking beers and talking shite, variations of people trying to sell us drinks and massages and fruit, the sun setting in front of us, across the water. We guess where the moon might rise from if it is to rise at all. And eventually, it gets cold enough to encourage us to leave the beach, and we wander towards Barceloneta in search of a bar to see where the night might take us.

DREAM: DIMENSION SHIFTER

We are looking for something. I'm not sure what—a key or a book or a room, perhaps. This isn't clear, nor does it feel important to know. We're on the grounds of a hotel I'm familiar with in Cork but in this context it isn't a hotel. It's more like an apartment complex. It's mostly empty. The hallways echo.

I know that I fancy one of the girls that's with us and that she also fancies me. Pre-contextual knowledge. She is played by a girl I know but do not fancy is real life, but again this does not register. We are on a sort of date within a group which suggests that I am younger here than I usually am—perhaps a teenager. I can tell this by how awkward I feel about being around her. She is somewhere else within the complex now with friends, waiting for us to return with whatever it is we're looking for.

My brother is with me. He is the same here as he is when I'm awake. In other dreams my family members are often played by people who are not truly family members. Mostly, this never strikes me as unusual. He is unloading his car—taking out a pop-up tent from the boot while he tells me about how his marathon went in Amsterdam at the weekend. He could have done it faster. His body didn't respond correctly. I feel proud of him, but am preoccupied by the thing we need to find even though I don't know what the thing is. If I delve deeper, which I do, I understand this preoccupation is a desire to get back to the girl I fancy, and I need to find the thing in order to do this.

Every door we try to open is locked except for the front door which is the door I stand in now as my brother unloads his car and tells me about his race.

Then suddenly we are outside in a sort of public green area between apartment blocks. The sun is shining and there is a barbecue taking place. There is also a small carousel nearby with those plastic horses for children to ride on. The typical monotone music associated with a circus is playing. I have no burning desire to ride the carousel which means I am not a child, but I know that I am not an adult either.

There are several dogs around. One in particular—a grey and white sort of terrier—catches my eye. I rush forward to pet it. It starts to growl aggressively as I stretch out my hand so I pull back. But it has already made its decision to attack and suddenly it is clenching down on my thigh, teeth baring, eyes vicious explosions. I feel fear. I do not feel any pain but this isn't enough in the moment to make me realize that I am dreaming. My brother comes quickly to get the dog away from me. Its faceless owner is apologetic and eventually we pry its jaws wide enough for me to get free. I feel the urge to kill this dog, but a moment later this urge passes.

We jump forward some time. I don't know how I know this, the knowledge is just present. I see the dog again and want to reconcile. I approach more gingerly, with my hand outstretched with a generic 'I come in peace' energy. The dog sniffs at my hand and seems to be lowering its head for me to pat it. As my hand descends it cranes its neck and latches onto my fingers, biting down again but this time on bare flesh. I shout out in pain but still feel nothing. I see blood. I feel people shouting nearby to get the dog off of my hand. Its grip is relentless. My visions goes blurry. And then I am no longer with the dog.

I am in bed. I haven't just awoken but I do not remember getting into bed. Now for some reason I know that I am dreaming. It becomes obvious that I am asleep, perhaps because I am in a bed in the dream. For whatever reason, I am lucid.

I am completely covered by the blanket so that my head is underneath and I am staring up at the patchwork design of the duvet cover. I used to do this a lot when I was a child. And suddenly I cannot breathe. I am suffocating. I gasp. I clutch at my throat and try to push the blanket off of me but nothing is working. The blanket is unmovable and I am dying. I am dying. The light is fading. The patchwork transforms from criss-crossing squares to thousands of eyes, blinking, lifeless eyes that are staring directly at me. And then I am screaming for help. I scream and bellow and the part of my brain that knows I am dreaming wonders if I am now shouting in my sleep. I shout and shout and after several long minutes of suffocation without dying I can hear my parents' voices through the screams. They are trying to wake me. I must be screaming in my sleep because they have come into my room to try and wake me. They sound scared. Perhaps I am having a seizure again, or have gone catatonic.

My vision begins to fade again and the eyes before me begin to darken and I wake up, suddenly upright on the floor. I am in my childhood bedroom in my parents' house but it is furnished differently than usual. There is almost no furniture. My bedroom door is open and across the hall is still the bathroom. But the floor is a crude unfinished concrete and the walls have that slimy looking paint you find in basements or old school bathrooms. There are bare pipes lining the walls and everything is cold. It does not feel like home but rather like somewhere I am being kept. Like I have been kidnapped and this is where I've been hidden away.

I feel much younger now. Although my legs are still tattooed, I look down at my body and understand myself to be around ten years old. I turn my head to where my bed is and my parents are both sat there, both visibly younger, too. The bed is made up as if no one had been sleeping there.

"Is this real?" I ask, confused and in a much different voice than I'm used to.

"Yes, of course. You were having a nightmare. It must be due to the medication," Mom says this and Dad nods along affirmingly, robotic. They are both smiling too much. I stretch out my ten year old arm and rub it with my other hand. I feel I still have an adult's brain and all the knowledge I have accumulated in my 28 years, but I am a child.

"They said night terrors might be a side effect," says Dad, still smiling. Neither of them reach out to comfort me. They just sit perched on my bed, looking down at me. They do not feel like my parents.

"I was suffocating. I couldn't breathe..."

As I begin this sentence the light begins to fade again and I can hear both this child's voice and my adult voice saying the words in unison. And I know now that I am talking in my sleep because I can hear myself, and I can feel the pillow beneath my head, and I can tell that I am waking up again.

I am back in the bed, back in the bedroom that is familiar. The room that feels like the correct timeline. I am not as scared as I have been with other nightmares. But there is an existential threat. I feel unsure of reality. I'd fallen asleep on my back again. The duvet is almost entirely off of the bed. I pinch myself several times in order to feel pain, to make sure I know I am fully awake, and not still in yet another layer of dream. There is confusion. I do not feel comfortable about falling back to sleep.

I think about the movie Inception. About how the characters carry totems that can tell them whether they are in a dream or not. I wonder about whether I should have one. These intense nightmarish experiences are happening more often now. I turn onto my side. I do not wish to fall asleep on my back again.

I check my phone. The time reads 1:19AM. I'd only been asleep for an hour. History suggests that I would forget this dream by the morning, but something deeper within me tells me that I won't. I wonder if I'll be able to fall back to sleep. My head is spinning. I'm not sure if where I am now is the real world, and I wonder where I'll wake up next.

OTHER POETS

Other poets tell me often about form and how important form is when constructing poems. I should always be considering form. Deborah Levy, in Things I Don't Want to Know, mentions that writers who are not ready to tackle form shouldn't concern themselves with it. Which leaves me somewhat between worlds. Because I'm ready, surely, but one could hardly say I'm motivated to tackle it.

Poems are their craft—so I understand. But my poems are not my craft. They are my feelings. And my feelings don't take the form of poems. How could they?

So I nod, and smile, and say thank you for the feedback. And I continue to write my feelings. And I continue to be left off of longlists and shortlists but this hardly matters. I have learned that one should not be competitive with their feelings, so I think other poets and I are doing entirely different things.

I am not a poet. Not in the way that gains praise from tastemakers at least. But I do write poems. And people do find solace in them. And I find meaning in their finding solace. I once heard Joe O'Connor say that the only writers who should write in a given genre are the ones who don't very much enjoy the genre. So perhaps this is me. A poet because I do not fully appreciate poetry.

To me, this is the only reason to write poetry—to try and

make sense of emotion. Not for awards. Not for placement in fancy publications. Not for bragging rights. Writing poetry is an exercise in finding connection. It is to let others know, and to let myself know, that we are not alone. Nothing else. Anything else is something else.

So maybe I am a poet. But not in the prescriptive way. Not in a way that other poets are.

Many literary essays start with commentary on a similar juxtaposition. They focus on the vulnerable and personal nature of writing and the bleak reality of getting published. Publishing being the commercial end goal of a process that is often the polar opposite of something to be commercialised. Writers bleed their souls, drop by drop, onto their pages for years at a time. For what? So it can be sold to the highest bidder. To me, it feels like a cynical conclusion to one of the purest things we do.

Often writers say that they would be writing even if they were never published. And it is mostly published writers who say such things. I've said it myself. But is it true? If, at the very beginning, you were guaranteed that your words would never reach an audience, never nestle upon bookshelves, never be read by eyes other than yours, would you still write? Would you feel the need to?

It is the same sort of expression as telling someone that you'd love to appear at their party when you know that you definitely, definitely cannot. You say it because you already have what you want. You have an excuse to say it. And so when we are published we say we'd still write even if no one read, because that reality is no longer one that is possible.

If we are purists then, we should write without the desire to be published. It shouldn't even be the last thing on our minds, it should be outside of it. Publishing, if it comes, should be a hinderance, a necessary obligation rather than a hopeful dream. Publishers should have to pull words from the writer's grasp like teeth. If we would really write if no one was reading then wouldn't we be reluctant for others to read?

Of course, this is nonsense. A thought experiment. A poor one at that. But as I was considering how unlike a poet I am I began to wonder what a writer is. Do you only become a writer, not the day you begin to write, but the day you begin to want your writing to be published? And if this is true, if a writer is someone who writes with the desire to be published, then is the claim that we would write even if we never published, false? After all we'd no longer be writers in this version of reality, we'd just be people who write.

So much of our identity is caught up in the fact that we are writers. We are writers first and foremost, everything else comes second.

There is a stylish ego within every writer. It flicks the wrist and thinks eternally, knuckles on chin, chin faced up. Our thoughts are more than the thoughts of others. It is never admitted to but it is proven by behaviour. The desire for people to read our words wouldn't exist if this was untrue. Our observations, considerations, perspectives come with an air of superiority. Please read these words, we say, because our egos need to breathe. The way we put thoughts together is unlike those who do not choose to write.

This ego: never accepted. Denied, understandably. It is a more subtle form of egoism, but it is egoism. A truth that rubs like sand on dry flesh. Uncomfortable like most truths are. We are not egomaniacs in the extreme sense, but we believe, at a level we wish to ignore, that we deserve to be heard.

Otherwise, what could possibly be the reason to sell best, to publish widely, to let the earth know that we, with our awkward stances and evading eye-contact, are writers. Published and validated. The truth refuses to settle for us—how could anyone so classically introverted house such an interesting ego?

That said, writers, poets, essayists are essential. I do believe that. They highlight a source of connection. They kindle compassion in a world that badly needs it. This ego that we never speak about is a fair price to pay for that. Of course there are bad players—elitists, gatekeepers—but there always is. They'll always be there, and they will always represent the darkest form a writer's ego can take. But we live with them, because whether we think of ourselves as writers and poets or not, the work is essential. The work is needed.

NOTE #2

Am I enough? I'm not good enough. I'm not good enough. I'm not good enough.

Yes you are.

No I'm not. Results speak for themselves. Can't deny the results. Over and over and over. Every Friday same thing. Unfortunately we cannot publish your work at this time.

Sure that's all part of it. That happens to all of us. You have to go through this part.

Do I? They didn't have to. They didn't struggle with this, struggle like this.

Yes they did, they just didn't talk about it like you do. The way you talk about it helps people. It lets them know that this happens to everyone.

Where's the proof for that? How do you know this happens to everyone? What if I'm the only one talking because I'm the only one who hasn't realised he's not good enough yet and given up?

Don't say things like that.

Why? Because it's true and you don't like to hear it? It's been years of this. Years of being rejected again and again. I can't take it, I can't handle it. I'm not as strong as you think I am. I feel like I'm spending all this time and my youth and giving up on a different life to pursue this one and what if I'm wrong? What if I'm not as good a writer as I think I am and everyone around me is just feeling sorry for me and telling me I'm good when I'm shite?

Don't say things like that.

Why? You said it was good that I talk about how hard this is and right now I'm on the verge of giving up and you're telling me not to talk about it? Can't have it both ways. Can't have both. All I want is to be granted the same opportunities the rest of them get. Not even considered, recommended, glanced at. My work is shit. It has to be. Otherwise they'd care. Otherwise they'd email with better news. But here I am. Alone as always and getting fucking nowhere.

But all those other people know the right kinds of people. They went to college and they met people. It's all about who you know. That's true of every industry.

So what? Even if my work is good enough it'll never go anywhere if I don't know the right people? That hardly seems just.

Well, life has never been fair. You know this. You speak about this.

Yes, okay but just for once, one time, I'd like if the universe could throw a guy a bone and be just, be fair, be with me rather than feeling entirely against me. Is that too much to ask for? I'm not asking for everything, just for something, anything, to come through, to work, to be felt, be seen, be heard. Can I ask for that? Is that too much? Am I being too much?

Bad days come. You're just in one of them now. It'll pass. It's not as terrible as you think. This will pass. I promise. Every bad day you've ever had has passed. You're good. You'll be good. You are good, you'll be good.

MY DIRECT MESSAGES INBOX IS A GRAVEYARD

My direct messages inbox is a graveyard. For all the conversations I never finished. All the talking stages that never amounted to anything more. All the forgotten beginning bits of relationship that never fully flowered. They're time capsules of a time I can't remember. Spitting up turns of phrase I'd never use now. I find them fascinating and repulsive simultaneously.

Once in a while, I'll type a random phrase into my direct message search bar and press Enter. Most recently I typed the words 'live in' and watched my screen fill with all the conversations that ever mentioned these two words. And there are so many, with people I can't even remember. Names I don't recognise, dots I cannot connect. But when I enter the conversations, I am there. A version of me at least. Not one I have a strong recollection of being. But I am there, and I am talking, and it is weird to perceive the past version of yourself in this way. Peering inside of interactions they thought were private. But they weren't, because I can see them. And while we are the same person, we're not really. He is a version I can no longer be, I am the version he is yet to become. And I wonder then if this exercise in viewing the old conversations is some sort of violation.

There are forgotten messages to women I can't remember. Attempts at light-heartedness, at flirting, at being something I'm not to impress people that would never like the real me. There are many messages I've forgotten to reply to. Other conversations where I have not been replied to. There are streams of memes and emojis. There is an entire life inside my direct messages. There are messages I cringe at, things said that I would never say now. Emotions. There is anger, there is cruelty. But there is also what appears to be the beginnings of what might be love. There are drunk misspellings and late night messages. There are question marks that float, reams of texts that were ignored despite my best efforts to start up conversation again and again. There is evidence of lives I lived and could have lived.

Sometimes when I have time to kill and I'm avoiding doing more productive things like reading, I'll scroll through my phone and pick at random these conversations. Some are so old, and were so brief, that I don't even recognise the connection. And yet, each time I go into chat conversations from the past, I see myself there, chatting with someone I at least knew to some degree at the time, forming a relationship with someone who has become again a stranger.

I scroll and enter chats, again and again, observing all the relationships and friendships I no longer have with these people. It feels like there is an infinite amount, all the people who touched my life that I'd erased from memory. With some, we no longer follow each other, cutting the only ties that connected our lives. Other people still follow me but I no longer follow them, others are the reverse of that. These details act like breadcrumbs, showing who scorned who, who was hurt most by the other person, or who got sick of seeing the other's face pop up on their screen without consent.

There are conversations though, that strike a memory, flinting a spark of the care I used to have for certain individuals. And there is a microscopic feeling of grief in me, I can taste it, for paths not chosen, or maybe more accurately, paths not considered interesting enough at the time by either party to bother walking down. It's an awareness of what might have been if we kept up our interactions, followed through on Sunday plans to meet up. Every choice made is also a negation of a thousand other decisions. A Multiverse exists in a way, inside my direct messages. It recounts all the paths I did and did not take, recording all the roads I could have walked down, but for one reason or another, did not. I see all the paths splayed out in text-threads, all the plans that were never kept, all the new loves that died off, all the what if's in digital pixelation.

And so I find this process both comforting and distressing. The names at the top of the list, the people I most frequently interact with, symbolise the roads I did choose. And the forgotten ones I find when I scroll symbolise the untaken paths. It's comforting on some days because it shows me the intangible in somewhat of a quantifiable pattern. Here are the people in your life, it says, here are the people you chose, and who chose you. And I can be grateful for the names I see popping up. On other days it can be distressing because I see all of the life I have not chosen. All the people that I do not walk with, either due to their choice, or my choice, or both. Lives that intertwined and crossed but never stayed together for too long.

So this is what I do, not very often, but sometimes. I enter the graveyard on my phone. I see the people I've wronged or hurt, the people who have hurt or wronged me, the friends who have become strangers, the would-be lovers who faded into the background, the new friends I've found, the acquaintances I'd forgotten, the life I carved out. It maps out an entire existence, this inbox. We forget how many people our lives touch. How many people's brain chemistry we've changed, if only briefly. We forget all the people that transformed our own lives, caused us heartbreak, made us laugh, cry. We forget it all because it's too much life to hold in one brain. But my phone holds it pretty easily, without attachment or pain. And so, every now and then, I scroll through it and look at all the people I've forgotten. All the people who may have left marks on my life, whose marks may still appear in me now, that I had forgotten to remember. And it feels like a funny thing, to remember them all again.

AFTER LYON

Lyon was much grittier than Barcelona. It's like the cast-iron frying pan that makes food taste better because it hasn't ever been cleaned properly. Lyon was and is the gastro-capital of France (allegedly), and also reminded me of home. It's a city set on a river split into two, and it is this specific quality that reminded me of Cork, making this alien place feel familiar.

Disembarking the train, I stepped immediately into the chaos of Lyonnaise France. People were shouting and running in all directions. There were whispers of confrontation and the tangy scent of engine fuel everywhere. The safety net of Barcelona vanished. Even in the train station, this new city screamed at me that it was not Barcelona and that it did not want to be. People barked at one another and weren't afraid to stare. Outside, a colossal city library towered over the train station like a vengeful God. It didn't look like a place people visited often.

It was 18 degrees Celsius and nobody at all was wearing shorts. Everyone seemed to be in a hurry. I wasn't sure of where exactly I needed to go and tried pathetically to ask passers-by for directions. My French was far better than my Spanish, but still the words stuck to my palate like chewing gum when I tried to speak. I tapped an address into my phone and headed in the direction it told me.

As soon as I started walking it became clear that Lyon felt

less safe than Barcelona. Perhaps this was because I didn't know anyone here, nor did I have an understanding of how the city was laid out. When something is unknown it automatically registers as scary or dangerous. I walked through litter-filled laneways which housed many boarded up buildings covered in graffiti. There were hooded men on street corners, old women carrying babies like bags of potatoes, smartly dressed couples, and an almost infinite number of electric scooter connoisseurs. Despite my unfamiliar surroundings I felt comfortable being amongst a population without knowing their language outright. It still felt like I was an outsider, but less so than if I was simply on a holiday. Lyon felt far less inviting, and therefore far more real to me than Barcelona. It felt the way Dublin sometimes did back home.

The hostel I'd chosen—Le Flaneur—was in a graffiti-riddled red-brick building with bars covering the windows in the south of the city. For a moment I thought it might have been closed down or that I'd mistakenly come to the wrong address. The doubts evaporated as I entered through the security door to find a smiling Frenchman with bleached hair welcoming me. He seemed genuinely happy to see me and already had my name stumbling from his mouth.

"This place," he insisted on telling me, "is run as a socialist endeavour, meaning there is no boss and all of the workers share the work equally."

I hadn't slept very well the night previous, having gone out for pints with Ben from Rosslare in Barcelona, and so I found myself feeling apathetic to whatever ideals he was trying to convince me of. I thought they might only be fooling themselves with this gimmick, or that maybe he was just trying to convince himself, but I kept the thought to myself.

Assigned once more to a top bunk in a hostel that wasn't as nice as the previous one, I abandoned my belongings in the corner of the room. I was tired and wanted sleep. I darted out quickly to grab a bite to eat before returning to my dorm to watch some comfort TV—specifically cartoons—and hopefully grab a quick nap. And it is here where I met Rejoy, a half-Indian, half-American lawyer who worked in Geneva, lived in Lyon, and had an unexpected love for Irish trad.

"Hey man, do you have my earphones?"

These were his first words to me. His tone was accusatory, his hair was long and black, his beard shorter and greying. He spoke with a sort of mongrel accent, partly American, partly British, partly German.

"I haven't a clue, man, sorry," I said, having literally just entered the room for the second time in my entire life.

He immediately let me in on his theory that the man who slept above him in the bunk had taken them because he'd already taken his jacket. This was his best available knowledge. There was no evidence for either of these robberies, obviously. He was wearing a jacket too, so I wondered about the alleged stolen one and whether it existed.

Following this interaction I clambered into my bunk and mostly ignored this strange man as he jerked around the room looking for his invisible earphones. He kept muttering 'Scheiße' under his breath. Soon I was asleep and he was gone.

After waking later that evening I made my way to the common room area of the hostel which doubled as a public bar. The place was buzzing with exotic sounding voices. I found my way to a table with only one other occupant—a pretty French girl eating pasta—and attempted to read a few more pages of the stubborn Infinite Jest. After maybe a page and a half I caught sight of a hand waving in the corner of my eye. It was Rejoy, the fella from my dorm again, sitting in a booth across from another man.

"Hey, Irishman, pint?" he gestured at the glass in his hand. After that, he'd never call me anything other than Irishman unless he was introducing me to someone new. My name tended to sound posh and out of place in his mouth.

I looked at him, the curl of a smile barely visible through his scruffy beard and I shrugged my shoulders.

"Why not?"

I closed the book I was more than happy to abandon, ordered a pint from the bar and joined my dormmate at his table.

He wore a grey duster jacket, one I would never see him without. His hair was almost shoulder length and patchy; he was self-conscious about losing it. He often ran his hands through his beard when he was speaking. The way in which he talked—his directness and his constant stream of questions—made him feel untrustworthy, as if he was searching for something he might want. His train of thought, and therefore conversation, jumped from place to place with minimal cohesion.

It was a Monday evening. He was due to drive to Geneva the following morning at 9:30AM. The reason I mention this detail is because I was surprised when he asked me if I wanted to get a bottle of whiskey with him after revealing his early departure.

"Do you want to get a bottle of Scotch?"

It was almost within a sentence that he asked, like he wanted to get off the subject of Geneva. Nevertheless, I agreed because, what else was I really doing? Soon we both returned from a short hiatus with a bottle of scotch. The way Rejoy pronounced the word 'scotch' sounded incredibly upper-class Brit and I surmised that he had either spent some time in Britain or learned how to say scotch in this particular way in order to sound sophisticated. My gut told me it was the latter but I never asked.

We drank for a time until another friend of Rejoy's joined us. Before long I was tipsy and chatting the ear off anyone who'd care to listen. I felt like I was someone new, that I was observing myself rather than actually living what was going on. Finding myself in these new situations surrounded by strangers, I felt sort of proud of my ability to adapt and roll with whatever was going on. It didn't feel like me, and in truth I didn't feel like myself, as if I was acting out the role I ought to be inhabiting.

That night ended with myself, Rejoy and his friend making a pilgrimage to a beautiful viewpoint of the entire city of Lyon. The whole night my gut told me that Rejoy was not someone I could trust. His energy was too erratic. He bounced from point to point like an angered hornet. He was impulsive and unpredictable. No one from home whom I trusted behaved in this way. But I wasn't at home, and the Irish way of being is far from perfect, nor is it universal. So I chalked Rejoy's nature down to a simple variety of being, and remained open to the possibility that he wasn't full of shit.

"I have a place I want to show you," Rejoy rejoiced, the twinkle of adventure swirled around his eyes with the scotch. He didn't say much more than that and instructed me to follow him.

It was raining out, but this didn't seem to affect his ambition. Not doing anything else, I followed. Night had fallen, the pavements were wet and empty. We crossed the river into the older part of Lyon where the streets were cobbled and lined with bookshops, cafes and tourist-trap restaurants. We then crossed a second bridge to the far bank of the river that arched into a hill where the Basilica and an old amphitheatre lay hidden. The rain was falling hard as our calves burned to ascend the hill. I had the neck of the half empty bottle of scotch squeezed in my fist. About halfway up the hill a small park emerged on the side of the road which Rejoy led us into. From there, we could see the entirety of Lyon, its lights twinkling in the rain, the sounds of its sirens and car engines and nightcrawlers floating up the hill towards us.

The viewpoint was unexpected. I wasn't sure where he was bringing me or why I followed. You could catch a full panoramic view of Lyon here from the far bank of the River Saone. We toasted a drink of what remained of the scotch upon the hill before heading back down. The rain never let up, reminding me once again of home.

We got back to the hostel around 1AM, our clothes drenched. I felt bad that Rejoy had to get up so early, seeing as I was certain I would be fairly hungover the next morning. Sleep found me soon after I found the pillow. It was the type of sleep you wake from more tired.

And indeed I was hungover the following day. I felt the force of an entire ocean of wasps inside my skull. I woke around 10AM with the dryness of alcohol consumption in my mouth, as well as the dull pounding of a daylong headache. Turning over I noticed that Rejoy was still sound asleep in his bunk below. I had been sceptical of his employment as a lawyer in Geneva to begin with, considering he lived in a hostel in Lyon and boasted about clearing 10k a month as a salary. When I saw him still dozing as I shook myself awake I concluded that this man had a proclivity for lying to strangers in order to make himself feel better.

I got out of bed and went for a run. I went back up that God awful hill we'd climbed the night before and I visited the amphitheatre and the Basilica at the very top. The views of the city were even more beautiful beneath the cold October's sun. The amphitheatre was ancient and the Basilica smelled of wealth. I clambered between them, gasping for breath and sucking in the cool autumnal air. I sat in among the stones that would have accommodated an audience centuries ago and tried to imagine what it would have looked like in its prime, a place to gather at the top of this hill overlooking the valley of an old river. I ran back across the twin rivers and found an outdoor bodyweight gym on the bank of the River Rhone, which I attempted to make use of before jogging back to the hostel. My muscles ached and screamed at me but I felt content stretching them out alongside the river, clearing my body of the residing hangover, clearing my mind of any anxious thoughts that were accumulating.

When I returned from my exploratory run around the city a good two hours later, Rejoy was only just getting out of bed himself, his hair dishevelled and a familiar look of discontent spread across his face.

"Didn't make it to work then?" I smirked at him as I re-entered covered in sweat.

He was rubbing his eyes like a sleepy toddler. "I texted my colleague. I'll go in tomorrow."

I nodded at him and headed for a shower. I had no problem spending time with this fella, but I definitely felt he was a chancer from there on.

After my shower I got to the common area for an hour or so to cook and do some work before our boy Rejoy emerged, the air of mischief at his feet. Once again, he'd caught me just as I began to read Infinite Jest, so I was happy for the bit of respite. Despite his untrustworthy nature I couldn't say he wasn't fun.

"Irishman, I'm heading out to the terrace for a cigar. Would you like to join me?" It was all very casual. He patted his breast pocket as if smoking cigars was the most natural thing in the world.

He lingered over me.

"Ah fuck it, why not," I replied.

I closed the book and tossed it into my backpack before following Rejoy out to the terrace. There were only a handful of other people out; two older Frenchmen smoking cigarettes and drinking cans of lager, and another French woman on the far side of the courtyard also smoking. We sat down at an empty table and Rejoy produced a fat brown cigar from one of the many pockets of his duster jacket and lit it up. He was in good form despite his hangover. We passed the cigar back and forth while Rejoy played some Irish trad on YouTube from his phone. He played The Dubliners and Sinead O'Connor and Raglan Road and some songs I'd never even heard of. One of the Frenchmen joined us, and although his English wasn't great he was more than up for the craic. The bottle of scotch from the previous night, which was almost empty, reappeared and we began to drink. Rejoy and the Frenchman gave their best attempt at an Irish jig and Céilí which I was happy to watch and record.

When we found the end of the bottle we three all went to a nearby supermarket to fetch another. This time I insisted on a bottle of Jameson, and seeing as the Frenchman appeared to have no money at all, Rejoy and I paid for it. Leaving the store, Rejoy slinked off to get a Covid test because he had plans for us all to go to a party that night and he wasn't vaccinated. So off he went whilst we made our way back to the hostel.

"Better safe than sorry, my friend," he said, and disappeared.

The terrace was more crowded upon our return. There was a large American man sitting at one of the tables. I knew he was American just from looking at him. He was chain smoking cigarettes and wore a Gillet jacket with shorts. His hair was short and blonde, his eyes blue and relaxed. His American-ness was palpable. I asked if he wanted to join us and he did without hesitation. He pulled over a seat and I offered him some whiskey.

"Christ, you're very American aren't you?" I said.

He laughed, "At least I have an international English accent though." This was a term I would adopt and go on to use despite not having one myself.

He spoke quickly in a kind of slow way. Much like myself, this American's French significantly improved once the hesitancy of sobriety wore off. Soon, he and I were speaking broken French confidently to the French woman who'd been on the other side of the terrace smoking earlier in the afternoon. She had no English, but we still managed to create some semblance of conversation. The intentions were good.

Soon enough darkness faded in but our energy levels were soaring as we worked our way through the bottle of whiskey. The terrace began to fill up too, as more productive members of society peeled away from their day jobs and came to the Flaneur Hostel for some drinks after work. It was during this busier period that she appeared; the girl from Venice who stood by the doorway with her hands in her jeans pockets and asked us if we had a lighter. She approached our table without any cigarettes and never actually followed up on the location of a lighter. This was how I met Isabella, the girl I would inevitably fall in love with.

She joined us, sitting down across from me at the table. Her English was good and not typically bent out of shape in the usual way. I wouldn't have guessed she was Italian. All I would have been able to say was that English wasn't her first language. She was beautiful, clearly, and I noticed the eyes of every man upon her as soon as she entered the terrace. Her eyes were a subtle, pale green and there was a confidence about her that was as rare as anything back home. She was enchanting and terrifying all at once. I couldn't tell you what we talked about then, but her smile was incredible and her laugh infectious. The attraction was glaring and immediate. I quietly hoped it was mutual.

"Do you want to come along to a party with us?" I asked on the end of sip.

"I leave Lyon tomorrow," she shrugged, "So I think it must be a quiet night for me." Considering the amount of eye contact that lingered between us, I wasn't convinced, and it didn't take much to change her mind about joining us.

When Rejoy eventually returned, myself and the yank had all but finished the bottle of whiskey. I introduced Rejoy to our new companions and gave him a hug before pouring him the last drink from the bottle.

"We got a wee bit carried away," I apologised.

"It's no problem, my friend," he said, taking the drink and looking at his watch.

He was restless, buzzing around the table like a wasp. He seem solely focused on getting us to a party, which was on a boat on the River Rhone. A friend of his was having a fundraiser for some charity—I'm not sure on the details—and he'd promised that he'd bring a handful of people—that was us. Earlier in the day I was reluctant to go due to a fairly prominent hangover, but after a feed of whiskey it seemed like a grand idea, especially now that Isabella had decided to join us.

"We better be off," Rejoy announced, finishing off his drink and standing. He'd sat for all of 30 seconds and hadn't bothered to remove his duster jacket. Off the four of us went, myself and Rejoy in the lead while the American and Isabella followed about ten metres behind us. I found myself looking back often to make sure they were still with us. We cut across the front of a McDonald's and skipped down the steps to join the walkway that ran alongside the river.

"It's not much further," Rejoy pointed to a group of boats docked a little further up the promenade.

We found the boat, docked permanently on the river, bobbing in the dark water. Rejoy's friend greeted us outside—entry was free but donations were strongly encouraged. As we boarded, Isabella mentioned she was hungry and I noted the opportunity. I was also quite hungry, not having eaten since lunchtime. We took a quick walk around the small vessel first. Inside there was a DJ's deck set up and the space was cleared to make a dancefloor, there was also a bar and a urinal tucked behind an outcropping for minimal privacy.

"We'll be back there in a few, Rejoy, we're absolutely starving, not eaten all day." And off myself and Isabella went.

I first kissed her on the steps we sat on looking out over the river, brown McDonald's bags splayed out between us. It was freezing cold as we huddled there in the middle of October. There was a pause filled with eye contact and there was a smile chasing her lips and then there was the kiss. It was nice the way important kisses are, and passionate and beautiful, the way movies make them look. We laughed awkward smiles and I squeezed her hand in the cold, and the drink we'd had before kept any anxieties at bay. I barely knew this girl but it didn't feel that way.

We returned to the party to re-join the others and danced and drank and smoked and laughed. Rejoy and I finished off the cigar from earlier overlooking the river from the back of the boat. The sun had already set, painting the sky a soft pink as we absorbed the night's air. Every so often my hand would find hers and she'd smile at me. It was the sort of smile that mocked whilst also telling you there was no one else in the room who mattered. We found ourselves stepping away from the group to sit and chat together. The way she said my name was intoxicating. She told me to call her Lucrezia in an exaggerated Italian accent and I told her to call me Mark if it was easier than the Irish jaggedness of my real name.

"What's your favourite colour then, Lucrezia?," I asked and she rolled her eyes.

"You are so stupid, Mark," she said before kissing my lips.

When we left the party, a Frenchman who looked like Timothy Chalamet tried to crack onto her over cigarettes. I wasn't worried but it was enough to gain my attention. Already she had the ability to make me jealous in the ways only a woman really can. The next day, and again on other days, he'd text her asking to meet up and she'd use this information to tease me.

"I'll fuck him if I get bored of you."

She threatened to fuck a lot of people, actually. Her idea of a joke.

Later that night—much later and after Chalamet had failed in his attempts—we returned to the hostel and had sex in the shared bathrooms. I had never done this before. We weren't legless enough to chance our luck in the small shared dorms with an audience of fellow travellers, so our drunken minds lead us naturally to the bathrooms. They were clean enough and empty, the lights a bit too bright for something so intimate. At one point another person came in and we had to be quiet in the stall we'd chosen. The sex was less enjoyable than it was symbolic, as if we both just wanted to claim the other as our own, marking our territory like feral beasts. As we re-dressed Isabella decided that we'd get a hotel the following day for one night and I had no objections to this at all. She pushed her plans to leave Lyon. I left her by the door to her room. It was around 3AM, and I was already falling.

I met her in a nearby café the following morning. We found a cheap hotel and spent the entire day in bed aside from breaking for food. We attempted a walk to a park nearby that Isabella recommended but, finding that we were too hungover and the park too far away, we returned to our room in the Hotel du Helder and got back into bed.

There was something between us I'd never felt before. We looked into each other's eyes and saw something familiar. I'd never felt so much in such a short space of time. After only knowing Isabella for 36 hours I felt I genuinely cared for her, and she for me. I wrote her poems and she placed kisses on my shoulder as we walked hand in hand along the streets of Lyon. She told me the meaning behind her tattoos and I told her about my writing and what I was trying to get it to mean. We bled openly to one another and we spent hours looking into each other's eyes. I didn't feel anxious when I was with her. She seemed to possess the ability to eradicate it. Neither of us wanted to leave the other but we were both due to leave Lyon a day later. When we went to bed that night I didn't want to fall asleep for fear of it all ending.

Morning eventually came. I walked her to a tram stop nearby so she could catch a train to somewhere else. Spain. She asked me to join her. Her eyes were big and wet then as she looked up at me. Her voice was on the precipice of imminent tears.

"I'm going to miss you," she cooed, her mouth pouted.

"I'll miss you too," I said, "but we'll see each other again soon, I promise."

A part of me wanted nothing else than to go with her into our adventure, but I knew I had to go north to Paris. We promised each other we'd meet again in Prague three weeks from then before she kissed me, stepped onto the tram, and disappeared from Lyon and from me.

I had a train to catch later the same day—a two hour high-speed journey to Paris. Returning to the hostel, I packed my stuff as I chatted with Rejoy.

"Do you like her?" he asked bluntly.

In the past I've usually hidden such things from the outside world. There was no uncertainty this time though, despite the somewhat elusive nature of her, and despite the jarring uncertainty that surrounded us.

"You should find a woman who is loyal to you," he continued before I could reply to his question. I didn't really understand what he meant by it. He idled by his bunk, pushing his shoulder-length thinning hair out of his eyes.

I left my bags at reception and we went to get a coffee before I left. Rejoy told me again as we walked.

"You never get your time back."

This was the lesson he so wanted to share with me. He'd been saying it all week. He was in a sort of sentimental mood I think.

"Some people come into your life, change everything and then you never see them again."

He posted a picture of me on his social media feed relaying the same message. I'm fairly certain he was talking about me, but I think, in a way, he was also talking about Isabella.

After our coffees he brought me to the metro and told me where to get off. The train station would be there. I thanked him for everything, and felt that in the end he was a good guy, despite playing on my instinct not to trust him from the outset. I sort of felt guilty for distrusting him so immediately, so assuredly, for summing him up so incorrectly. All he wanted was for people to enjoy themselves, and to make the most of their time. I'd been projecting my fears of being robbed or taken advantage of onto him. So many people had warned me of such things happening to solo travellers, and I realised here how tense I had been when I'd met Rejoy, how immediately distrusting I was. As Connie had taught me in Barcelona, leading with this mindset would only bring these fears to fruition.

He mentioned a few nice places to eat near where I was saying in Gard du Nord in Paris before shaking my hand firmly and skipping back up the steps to the street, disappearing as quickly as he'd entered my life. And as I waited for the underground train to come I found myself alone for the first time in days. I could feel that I was alone. When I left Ireland I anticipated spending most of my time alone, but so far the opposite had been true. I was constantly surrounded by people, strangers weaving their lives into mine and becoming temporary friends and lovers. It was unexpected, and so being alone felt uncomfortable rather than expected.

I KEEP HAVING DREAMS OF ALTERNATE REALITIES.

In many of them I am happier than I am here. My back isn't always so sore. I don't feel so insecure, so filled with pressure like my heart's about to burst, I've been having chest pains for years but hopefully they'll just go away once I hit the next goal. After the next achievement I'll be happy but this is never true. In the other places I stare at the sky and this is enough. I'm jealous of how simple it could be. I have memories that don't belong to me, like I snuck into the back of a theatre and stole some art. Sometimes I nap just to disappear into another life for an hour and change. Funny how we fear death but love sleep, two branches of the same plant. It's not nothing, you see, the end. It's not nothing. You become nothing here to experience every other path you could have walked. And sometimes, if we're lucky, we get to walk these roads while we're still here. We oscillate between worlds, exist in both simultaneously. And every time I do this, I am jealous of how simple it can be to find peace.

But then remembering, and the knowledge of being remembered, are gifts. I know this because they can be taken away. Memory is a privilege. Sometimes we can get to remember, dreams, people, scents, feelings. But mostly we forget them. And people forget us. And so when I remember you I always send a text, just to let you know. Because knowing that someone has remembered you, somehow, someway, is a beautiful acknowledgement. And in the dreams I remember people I've never met, leading lives I'll never observe. There's more room inside than there is to etch memories on skin. I can't hold everything, but sometimes I can. And this is divinity, isn't it?

I know I'm not feeling well because simple disappointments are devastating. Like I'm so easy to shake from security. Another woman sent another text to cancel a date last minute. Normally this is just something that happens, but on Sunday it ruined my day and I drank too much to try and drown the feeling. On Monday I didn't work. I didn't feel like me. The sadness furrowed inside my arteries and pulsed around my body. I couldn't even write, but I did wonder. Should I be this vulnerable? All it does is cause pain. Pain for me but also pain for others. My mother rings more often without me telling her a thing. Mothers just have a sense that their children are in distress. I thought I'd stop being sad in a place where the sun is always out. But really, it just works to juxtapose how bad things are, being dark in a bright place.

Since arriving back here, to my new home, I have felt unanchored. We always think distance will make the problems smaller. But they come along with us. They hide between the rolled pairs of socks and headphones. No one looks up at the moon and feels pity for it, we have to imagine a man up there before we can consider it to be a lonely place. I often wonder if lonely places can feel their own loneliness, if it seeps into the consciousness within it. I can't feel the way others do, I always feel without, unanchored, floating. Like the moon. And so I think it must feel like a lonely place because we are the same, and I feel empty most of the time.

I don't mind if people unfollow me for the most part. Social media, ultimately, is not real. I do, however, care when people I like choose to opt out. Because it feels more pointed. People I know, who I have cared about, choosing to remove me from their digital lives is upsetting. And I don't want to pretend that it isn't. Often it is women I used to have some sort of romantic intertwining with. Things that didn't work out. And I understand their desire to remove me, to move on, to forget about me. But this understanding doesn't stop it from stinging. Some of them, I let down. I understand their disdain. Feelings left me and I never told some of them, I just faded and we stopped talking. Sometimes I am given out to. 'You never texted me,' as if it is my sole obligation to start conversations. But they never texted me either. They refused to text, let ego and pride stop them from doing so. So when things fizzle, it is my fault somehow, rather than a shared blame. And it is always a shared blame, but pride shrouds this truth from us. And so when another woman from my past unfollows, I understand, but I do feel hurt. I haven't always been a good man. I have never claimed to have been so, either. I'm trying to be better. And I think this trying, is uncharitably taken as a claim that I have always been good, always had integrity, always been upstanding. And I have not been. But they see me trying and think it means I am trying to ignore any misdeeds. I see my mistakes and accept them, but I refuse to settle on the past.

Here's the thing. I am trying to live in the light. Desperately, I am trying. Leading people on is not good for anyone. It hurts them, it hurts me. I become a person I do not like. I am working against my nature, to live in the light. I know this. I don't wish to dismiss my transgressions. They plague me, keep me up at night, cause me self-contempt. So if you feel I have not been punished for what I have done, or not done, I have. If I turned cold on you, this has never been personal. If I suddenly felt different, shifted energy, without communicating, I acknowledge this. I should have given you the respect of an explanation. I've always run from the hardness of a difficult conversation. It is easier for you to hate me without my knowing than it is to let you down firmly. This is weakness. I have been weak. I know this. You deserve more, and I should be better. I am trying to be better.

TO BE CREATIVE

Recently I attended the West Cork Literary Festival in Bantry, Cork. I was excited because it was my first time being part of the line up, but also because there were many incredible writers flocking to West Cork, too. I jumped in the car and went down a day early with the hope of soaking up as much inspiration as I could fit into my notebooks. Often when I attend literary events, I come away with something. Motivation or ideas or affirmation. A few months ago I attended a reading by Max Porter and the next day I was highly inspired, writing 28 pages of poetry in as many hours.

One event I attended at the festival discussed the role of the creative in addressing the climate crisis. There were both creatives and scientists discussing this important topic. During this discussion I was struck by something the poet Annemarie Ní Churreáin said. She said that, 'the role of creative is to be present, to draw others into the present moment.'

This thought has stuck with me, mainly because I think it's true, but also because I've never thought about creativity in this way before. Much of being creative is doing. It is not thinking or procrastinating, it is doing the thing, whatever your thing is. Art, poetry, novels draw us into the 'now'—the past fades away, the future is something irrelevant. If you think back to anytime you've consumed a good book, movie, poem, you find that you were absorbed in it. Your mind wasn't elsewhere. It was right here, right now. Good writing, good art, brings us directly into the present mindfully. We are emerged in only the moment that lays before us now.

Secondary to that, being creative provides a similar phenomenon. When we are creating, writing, crafting, painting, we are in this moment and this moment alone. We're flowing. Time no longer exists. Hours feel like minutes and days zoom by. The past is shrugged off. Anything on the horizon of our mind remains there. So it is clear to me that creativity—both the consumption of and participation in—causes us to live in the moment. And I don't believe this to be the side product of creativity. I think it is, in fact, the primary function of being creative.

Whenever I write a poem, I tend to write about how emotions feel in my body right now. Not how they felt earlier, or how they will feel later. It is the present feeling. The only version of it that actually exists. Annemarie, when she spoke, was talking about how creatives draw readers and viewers into the present. We guide people to look at the world as it is now, to experience the world they exist in now.

Our world, as it feels to me, is designed to force us out of the present. We can focus on the future or the past well enough, but being in the present is entirely difficult. When I look at my own life this holds true. Schedules fill up and future dates are marked for oncoming commitments. When I've achieved things—book launches, marathons, publications—my mind isn't focused on the present feeling of the achievement. It is looking to the next thing, the next goal, the next ambition. Phones are ever-present and take us away from what we're doing in the moment. Conversations are half-heard as thumbs scroll haphazardly through reams of information that constantly seek our attention. Attention is now a commodity. Corporations makes millions from gleaning outrattention away from us. It's a constant battle we all face—the desire to be in the moment versus the forces trying to take us away from it.

Living in this way, upon reflection, feels surreal. Literally unreal. Too much time spent away from the present begins to make life feel artificial and half-lit. My brain is constantly thinking of anything aside from what's in front of me, in the present. Constantly turning over to-do lists and schedules and places I need to be in the next few weeks. Spending time watching how other people live rather than living myself. None of which has any influence on the present. I could be in the present, but I'm hyper-focused on the future. And I'm not the only one. In fact, the majority are in this boat with me. Rather than appreciating the now, we're anticipating the hypothetical better tomorrow. We're always one minute, one hour, one month ahead of ourselves. We're living life looking backwards or forwards, but rarely are we living it live, as it happens.

It is a conundrum. The creative is supposed to draw the world into the present, but the world the creative lives in drags them out of it. And while this may have detrimental effects on the creative's craft, I think it has far weightier outcomes for a person's wellbeing.

It is rare, but when I am totally present, experiencing the now, being mindful, being attentive, this is when I am happy. This may even be the definition of happiness. Because when we are present, we can't worry about what may happen, or what could happen. it cuts out any threatening anxieties. Being present also means that I am unlikely to focus on painful memories from the past, or on mistakes I've made, or on regretful behaviour. Which means that the likelihood for me to fall into low mood or self-contempt is also quite low. When we live in the moment, the rest of our lives cannot affect us. The past cannot haunt, and the future cannot loom over.

So while it is the job of the creative to draw others into the present, how do we draw ourselves into the present, too? Doing the work, it is clear, helps. And 'the work' is far more than sitting at the computer to type and type. Living as a creative means you are constantly open to inspiration. You are observing, you are absorbing. When you are living your life you are still in the creative process, because it is from life that we write and create. So, in this sense, to be creative—to live creatively—is to attempt being present as much as possible. It's an aspiration, which means we don't always succeed, but living with the goal of trying to be present brings it about more often than if we lived without this goal.

If you are reading this and you don't lead a traditionally creative life—through the arts, writing, painting, sculpting etc.—then you might feel that I'm implying only these people can achieve living in the moment, or that maybe this essay is just for those types of people. But this is far from true. Because to be human is to be creative. It is our niche. The same way bees collect pollen to create honey, our desire to create is built-in, ingrained, genetic. Even when we aren't creating art, we are still always creating and being creative.

Everything we do as people has a creative element to it. Finding new ways to do menial tasks is creative. Cooking is creative. Gardening is creative. Taking a different route to get to a destination is creative. Picking out what clothes to wear is creative. Starting a business is creative. Creativity is something we all take part in a consistent daily basis, but we don't think of it like this. Some time ago, I don't know when, the arts monopolised creativity, and we began to believe that the only way to be a creative person was to engage with a specific artform. We narrowed down what it means to be creative to these narrow, albeit extremely important lanes. But you, and I, and everyone you know are creative intrinsically because we are human.

When I reflect on why I write I find myself realising that it's to keep me in the moment. Some of the writing is published in books, newspapers, journals, but the vast majority isn't. Most of the creative work is to help me to notice, to be aware, to be here. It is to realize that life is happening now—not later, not before—now. Being creative on a daily basis helps me to understand that. There are of course, other ways to achieve the same thing. Meditating, for one. But for me, the most effective, the most consistent is creativity. Be it participating or consuming, having creative elements throughout the day allow me to focus on the present rather than being somewhere else.

And so, if to be creative is to be present, then we each have the opportunity each day to attain it. We can choose to lean into the more creative elements of our lives to be present, to find flow, and to let the past and the future remain where they should. Traditional creatives might be tasked with drawing the world into the present, but each of us has the power to remain in it. And we can do this by finding space for creativity, even in the smallest details of our lives.

MY DEALINGS WITH THE ILLUMINATI

When I get the first message from The Illuminati to join The Illuminati it does not come as a surprise. I am exactly the kind of person that The Illuminati would recruit. They make a point of ensuring they are not an evil organisation. This is exactly the kind of thing an evil organisation would say. I ignore this first email. Because I couldn't be arsed replying.

Then there comes the DM from a man named Albert Hermann who only recently made his account. Which is suss, obviously. But I play along.

His first message goes like this:

> ILLUMINATI INVITATION:
> Based on the membership criterion of the illuminati, we find you are of great interest in possession of good mastery of manual dexterity and academic proficiency. With this, we look at you as the class that will be the platform for which you stand to meet wealthy people who can raise you to wealth, power, fame and glory.
>
> You have been chosen for greatness and empowerment and I Strongly recommend that you join us in the illuminati. Joining us you become wealthy and live the life you desire. Do you accept the offer?'

Of course I want to accept the offer. Nobody has ever bothered to notice my mastery of manual dexterity before. I am hooked. I just need to work out the details of my involvement. One of the key tenents to this organisation is that it is secret. Nobody can know you are a part of it. So I screenshot this message and put it on my story.

Albert goes on and on telling me about the purpose of the Illuminati. It's quite tedious and repetitive. I would have thought the Illuminati would be keen on efficiency and succinctness, but alas, it wasn't so. In short, they want to protect the human species from destruction by doing unclear things in the background of society. He doesn't give specifics, but I conclude that this is classic Illuminati behaviour. However, he does mention that joining isn't complicated, which I am happy to hear, because not too long before this encounter I tried to join a Spanish bank and that was extremely complicated. I am looking for an easy win.

After a long process of convincing Albert that I am serious, he gives me the key to joining:

> 'The Grand Master is a noble man and you will be blessed to talk to him.
> You can reach out to him on WhatsApp because he is a busy man, he will give you some other informations you need to know and guide you on how to become a member. You must have WhatsApp, right?'

He is right. I do have WhatsApp and he gives me the number, which I save in my phone as 'THE ILLUMINATI'

The Grand Master's name is Martin Davidson. I open our conversation:

> Hey GM, Albert sent me

An hour and a half later he messages me back:

> Hello, Greetings to you
>
> This is Martin Davidson, the Grand Master of the Illuminati. I'm glad to be in touch with you today. You're welcome to the place of breakthrough and a total turn around, so please do you want me to send all the information about the illuminati to you email address because I'm sending bulk messages to enable you understand what this is all about and we can discuss on here?

Of course, I say, and give him one of my emails.

This isn't unusual behaviour. Often, I reply to Nigerian millionaires desperately looking for someone to take their fortunes from them. It must be tough. I like to troll them, have conversations, see if I can make them give up.

But I've also been scammed successfully in the past. I was catfished not so long ago, had my nude images used against me in blackmail. I never paid, and the pictures were never leaked, but still, I was duped into thinking the person I was sending my pictures to was a real and trustworthy person but this was not the case. I understand it's a dangerous game to be playing. And the only reason I can see for doing it is that I think it's funny. It's that simple. I risk being blackmailed because I think the interactions are gas.

Anyway, back to Martin. It takes him a full day to email me, but when he does, I hit the shadow government jackpot. Email after email after email, thick with text about what The Illuminati does, and doesn't do. Again there are no real specifics, other than pontification about protecting the human race, selecting the few among us who are destined to lead etc. etc.

Here's an example:

> Welcome! We are delighted that your life's journey has led you to discover our organization. Maybe you have met one of our members in the flesh. Or perhaps not; we value anonymity. We see and know all just as a shepherd sees and knows all of the flock, our eyes peering over the masses to identify any threat. We are the bringers of new dawns, the guardians of the human species. We are the pyramid, the eye, the eternal. We are the Illuminati. The Illuminati is a collective of prominent figures throughout the world who have united to guard the human species from extinction. Our members bear the burden of a planets leadership with the lives of 7 billion in their hands. As the human continues to rise above its other animal counterparts governing of the planet has turned into a daunting task. In return for their loyalty, our members are presented a life of limitless wealth and opportunity.

There is an incredible footnote at the bottom of one of these nonsensical emails:

> NOTE; THERE ARE NO BLOOD OR HUMAN SACRIFICES IN THE ILLUMINATI.

And here I thought that's what they were all about. Their PR team is doing a horrendous job.

More ominously, Grand Master Martin Davidson implies that there are people around me who are already in The Illuminati, and that these people had highlighted my existence to the organisation for recruitment:

> The illuminati has members around you who have chosen
> you because they have came in touch with you one way or the
> other and have seen you as a man with a bright future but you
> won't know because of the secret legacy of the organisation.
>
> We are here to help and give you the necessary support
> and empowerment you need to better your career and
> endeavours and make you great, so you can have enough for
> yourself and also be a helping hand to those around you and
> life the best life you desire.

It's all very detailed without giving any actual detail, reminding me of things like horoscopes—telling the reader flattering things without actually saying anything of substance.

And then we get to the good part.

The final email I receive from Martin is a list of benefits that come with joining this secret organisation. Despite not being clear on what exactly would be required of me upon joining, they are very specific about the benefits:

BENEFITS GIVEN TO NEW MEMBERS
WHO JOIN ILLUMINATI:

1. A Cash reward worth $4,000,000
2. A New Sleek Dream CAR valued at $300,000
3. A Dream House bought in the country of your own choice
4. One Month holiday (fully paid) to your dream Tourist destination.
5. One year Golf Membership package
6. A V.I.P treatment in all Airports in the World
7. Golds
8. A total Lifestyle change.

I'd never seen a list so specific and so vague all at once. The fact that they have the funds to give me four million dollars in cash but can only manage to get me a one-month holiday and a one-year golf package is insane to me. I do, however, appreciate the vagueness of item 7—Golds—which could mean many golds or just a handful of golds. The possibilities are boundless.

The benefits are alluring. Especially considering I am perpetually without money, trips to the golf course, and golds. The housing market also makes the offer of a Dream House quite appealing. But I'm not convinced. Interestingly though, is that up until this point neither Albert nor Martin has asked me for anything. Usually in scams there is some sort of low administration fee they need to pay in order to transfer funds. I wasn't asked for any. All I had to do was sign over my soul for all these delicious benefits. It seems like the deal of a lifetime.

All that said, I don't bother replying. But I don't block them either. A few days later, Martin wishes me a good day on WhatsApp and asks if everything is alright because he hadn't heard from me in a few days (what a sweetheart). Later that same day, Albert DM's me on Instagram with a similar sentiment, solidifying my suspicion that Martin and Albert are in fact, the same person.

However, that same night, deep into the morning, I make the decision to block all parties. At around 2AM, while I am asleep, my phone starts vibrating violently on my bedside table. I wake up alarmed and confused, immediately thinking one of my friends or family members is in trouble. I pick up my phone to see the words, 'THE ILLUMINATI Is Calling' and silence the vibration. I know this is the beginning of non-stop hounding, so I block the number, and block Albert on Instagram before going back to sleep.

All things considered, it's a nice thought, knowing The Illuminati are desperate to recruit me, but I won't join no matter how many Golds they offer.

ACKNOWLEDGEMENTS

I hate writing these. Namely because you invariably always forget something. It's not that I hate thanking people – it's actually quite the contrary – I hate the idea of forgetting to thank someone.

I want to thank Aaron Kent and everyone at Broken Sleep Books for taking this book on. Some of my favourite writers have been published with you, and so it was, and is, a dream to join their ranks. With that in mind, I'd like to thank Lucy Holme, who has been a great friend, wonderful help, and thoroughly kind throughout the process of getting this book ready.

To every single magazine, publication, vibe-curator to publish my work over the years, thank you. I'm lucky to say there are too many to name. But without your encouragement, I wouldn't have kept going.

To my literary friends, who allow me to vent frustrations and condemn the gods in confidence. Patrick Holloway, Christine Anne Foley, Gary Grace to name a few. Thank you also to my essay critique group co-conspirators. Joining *The Yessayists* has improved my essays tenfold, and this book is far stronger because of your thoughtful feedback.

I wrote a lot of this book while living in Barcelona. The city has such a rich creative scene. It's been inspiring to be a part of it, and I owe a lot of gratitude to so many people who make it what it is.

To my family and friends outside of writing, you have shown superior patience with me, always. I can be difficult at the best of times. Thank you for giving me the space to be myself, even when it isn't pretty.

And finally, to everyone who supports the work. Whether that's by reading my work, listening to my poetry on social media, tuning into my various rantings online, showing up to performances in real life – thank you. Genuinely. It will never stop amazing me that so many people watch, read, listen. It means more than you'll ever know, I imagine.

LAY OUT YOUR UNREST